Flexible Higher Education

SRHE and Open University Press Imprint

Current titles include:

Flexible Higher Education

International Pioneers Reflect

Edited by Liz Burge

Society for Research into Higher Education
& Open University Press

Open University Press
McGraw-Hill Education
McGraw-Hill House
Shoppenhangers Road
Maidenhead
Berkshire
England
SL6 2QL

email: enquiries@openup.co.uk
world wide web: www.openup.co.uk

and Two Penn Plaza, New York, NY 10121–2289, USA

First published 2007

A catalogue record of this book is available from the British Library

ISBN-10 0335 217761 (pb)   0335 21777X (hb)
ISBN-13: 978 0335 217762 (pb)   978 0335 217779 (hb)

Library of Congress Cataloging-in-Publication Data
CIP data has been applied for

Typeset by RefineCatch Limited, Bungay, Suffolk
Printed in Poland by OZ Graf. S.A.
www.polskabook.pl

The **McGraw·Hill** Companies

Contents

Acknowledgements

First, a big thank you to colleagues around the world who reviewed the publication proposal for this book, responded frankly and helpfully to my squeaks of enquiry and doubt, or answered the Social Sciences Humanities and Research Council of Canada's request to critically review the grant application. To Professor Margaret Haughey goes a special thanks, not only for her Foreword, but also for her wonderful colleagueship over many years. I would like to interview you all one day!

Next, my deep appreciation goes to the trusting and hospitable participants whose contributions in the interviews made half of this book. They took time and energy to consider their answers to the interview questions before their telephone rang or I walked through their door.

Managing the flow of 46 transcripts during the stages of transcription, my minor copy-editing of transcripts before return to participants (since thinking-aloud speech is rarely comfortable to read), and monitoring the schedule of amended returns was a major task. Joyce Kennedy skilfully organized the flow with barely a blink.

The seven commentators were asked to read the Chapters in Part 2 and develop a response. Not an easy task. Thank you for your wit, skill and commitment to helping readers engage in critical meta-reflection.

Dr Jo-Anne Elder used her own publishing and teaching experience to keep an eagle eye for infelicitous writing. To read her unsolicited comments about interesting chapters giving her new insights was encouraging.

Thank you, Shona Mullen, Commissioning Editor of the Higher Education list and General Manager of Open University Press/McGraw-Hill Education, and Jennifer Rotherham, Editorial Assistant for the Higher Education list, for your professional guidance and consistent courtesy, not to mention the speedy processing of the original proposal.

Last, but absolutely not least: this research project was funded primarily from Grant 410–2004–0083 of the Social Sciences Humanities and Research Council of Canada (www.sshrc.org).

Liz Burge
Fredericton, N.B., Canada
December 2006

Foreword

Baron Crowther's definition of openness 'to people, to ideas, to places and to methods' provides a philosophical framework for this book and informs our understanding of the remarkable people Liz Burge has interviewed. No doubt a tremendous amount of work went into the creation of this book. Talking with 46 people in various continents, making travel arrangements to meet them where they felt most comfortable being interviewed, transcribing, listening, writing, reviewing, consulting with her interviewees, and then rewriting and editing all occurred; but the remarkable result is that we are not aware of these activities. Instead, we are introduced to the speakers, get a wonderful sense of their personalities, and carry those images forward as we hear their voices in interaction with Liz's analyses.

The world of distance education continues to be transformed. Yet, while digitization has brought many changes, and what was once marginal is now touted as mainstream, some things do not change. Most evident among these are the deeply-held values that run throughout the text. They reconfirm why we are distance educators: the interviewees speak passionately about the importance of providing learning opportunities, their sense of social justice, and their desire to ensure equitable access for all. Another value, presented by many different voices, is the desire to 'honor the students' perspectives', to consider their concerns, to listen to their needs, and to include the most marginalized, whether by place, or funding, or formal education, or access to various technologies.

I took away from my reading the importance of the interactivity between and among the learners, the course materials, the technologies and the learner support services. The descriptions of the early days in distance education when these interviewees were inventing models for course development and working in role-differentiated teams brought rich reminders of the excitement and challenge of those times. However, interviewees warn about the inadequacy and misguidedness of overly focusing on course materials without taking the other aspects into account. They speak about the importance of facilitative feedback to learners, of engaging with them, and of encouraging 'a generosity of spirit' in the approach of instructors, tutors and learners, a point reflected in Professor Börje Holmberg's theory on the importance of empathy towards students for course developers and tutors. Recently, I heard Professor Otto Peters speak about his model of distance education that has come to be associated with industrialization and, to his deep dismay, to even promote such a view. 'It is a model about pedagogy', he reaffirmed, noting that the disaggregation of the teaching act is one of the characteristics of distance education. In many ways his concern that we focus not only on the components of distance education but also equally on their integration is reaffirmed in the voices of these experienced practitioners.

The past 50 years have been a remarkable period for developments associated with all forms of radio and television. The stories about these practitioners' involvement with these media and the strategies they used to develop educational applications, especially in situations where there was minimal infrastructure, are engaging and inspiring. However, while they saw the advantages of these technologies for learning, some were much less supportive of online learning. I think it looked too close to traditional education models and hence their cautiousness.

There are several places where the interviewees speak about institutional management and the challenges not only of inventing and implementing a model within their organizations but also the challenges of gaining acceptance of distance education as a legitimate form of education by peer institutions, government bureaucrats and influential politicians. That they were successful is evident today in mainstream institutions' desire to be involved in distance education. The struggles to achieve this and the challenges they faced were personally and professionally demanding. Sometimes, as various practitioners recount, they were too difficult; for not only was distance education a different form of education but it also required a different form of institution, both of which threatened the status quo. In leading their organizations, strategic awareness of internal and external changes in context was essential; equally important throughout the stories was collaborative and collegial relations among professional colleagues both inside and outside the organization. These remain fundamental concerns for distance education organizations, where the pull to the norm is always present.

Besides stories and reflections on past practices, these experienced professionals identify concerns that have much to say to today's practitioners. They identify changes in today's learners, noting that they are more likely to be younger with fewer life experiences, less likely to be grateful for the opportunity to study and more likely to demand quality services at a price they can afford. They see course design models as changing from high-quality, team-based course development models to more flexible resource-based online options. In essence, course design is changing from telling students how to learn to giving them the tools to do it themselves. The interviewees note the blurring of former institutional boundaries and the acceptance of distance education as another form of educational provision. They express major concerns about the somewhat variable quality of the online learning models that are growing in prominence. They worry that the development of 'high quality learning materials' is being taken for granted, that flexibility in terms of pacing is being lost and that the provision of student support is assumed. They also point out the need for policies concerning foundational funding if distance education is to be properly supported and their concern that those mainstream institutions now adopting distance education practices seem unaware of the social justice concerns that they held, and still hold, dear.

There is much to learn, to remember, to marvel at, to enjoy and ultimately to ponder over. Ultimately, for those whose values echo those of the interviewees, the message is clear: we are not out of the woods yet! We must continue to model Baron Crowther's philosophy of openness 'to people, to ideas, to places and to methods'.

Professor Margaret Haughey
Vice-President, Academic
Athabasca University
Canada

Being autobiographical: who's who

The researcher and editor

The magic of reading a box of international children's books sent monthly from the State Library of South Australia to **Liz Burge** was later transformed into a profound respect for free and easy access to information. That respect has helped drive her careers in librarianship, instructional design, distance mode course design, teaching skill development and, at the University of New Brunswick in Atlantic Canada, professing adult and distance education. Her graduate students learn that questioning their own assumptions of practice and looking for hegemonic thinking are often not as cognitively painful as expected. Decades of technology adoption experience prompt Liz's current concerns about equitable access to information and context-appropriate, non-seductive use of technologies. For more information about Liz's work, see www.unbf.ca/education/faculty/burge.html

The commentators

Having completed a commerce degree at Liverpool University, **Michael Collins** headed for 'swinging' London to work in sales and business systems. Subsequently, and in search of mountains to climb and rivers to paddle (rather than career advancement), he emigrated to Canada. Enlightenment dawned when he attended a graduate class on adult education. Fulfilling work as an adult educator in urban and rural settings was followed by more graduate studies, leading eventually to his current job as Professor of Adult and Continuing Education at the University of Saskatchewan in Canada. His critical theory interests stem from a concern to illuminate what undermines the emancipatory aspirations of adult education and to engage in political action towards their achievement. To learn more about Michael's work, see www.usask.ca/education/people/collinsm.htm

The educational conveyor belt carried **Sir John Daniel** through ancient schools and universities for 22 years before dropping him into an academic post in metallurgy. Thinking to develop his teaching skills he enrolled in a part-time master's in educational technology. A programme internship at the UK Open University was a conversion experience that led him to join Quebec's Télé-université and re-orient his career to distance education. This led on to management and leadership posts at four other universities (Athabasca, Concordia, Laurentian and UKOU) and two intergovernmental agencies (UNESCO, Commonwealth of Learning). During his professional career he has completed the equivalent of three years' full-time study in distance learning courses from both dual-mode and single-mode universities. To learn more about Sir John's work, see www.col.org/colweb/site/pid/2833

After various creative forays into different fields of education, **Yvonne Hillier** eventually found her true home in adult and further education. She is now Professor of Education in the Education Research Centre of the School of Education of the University of Brighton, UK. She has worked on professional development programmes for practitioners who work with adults in all settings from prisons and police training to voluntary organizations and large local government institutions. Her research follows her interest in the post-compulsory sector and her passion is still focused on encouraging practitioners to work reflectively and test their ideas boldly. Some running (slowly), some backpacking, and some grandchildren enhance her own extensive reflection and writing. For more information on Yvonne's work, see www.brighton.ac.uk/education/contact/details.php?uid=ygjh.

Michael Grahame Moore is Professor of Adult Education at the Pennsylvania State University and his other interests include being the founding editor of *The American Journal of Distance Education*. Although he has been practising and writing about distance education longer than anyone else in this book, Michael still enjoys an active professional life that centres on his doctoral students face-to-face and masters students online, as well as consulting and conference presentations. He enjoys spending summers and any other time with his wife in their apartment in Devon, UK; giving him time to watch cricket, rugby, visit National Trust properties and eat Cornish pasties. For serious stuff, he asks you to visit the *Journal*'s website, at www.ajde.com

After electrocuting himself and slashing his thumb in lab sessions at university, **David Murphy** decided that engineering was not for him and retreated to the far safer world of mathematics. Drifting into teaching, he found himself dropped unexpectedly into distance education. A few years later, via a record number of postings to Hong Kong, he became a serial job-hopper. Between 1985 and 2005, he survived a Ph.D., enjoyed three jobs in Hong Kong (for a total of 15 years, 8 of which were in two stints at the Open University of Hong Kong) and three jobs in Australia, finally becoming the

Director of the Centre for the Advancement of Learning and Teaching at Monash University (see www.calt.monash.edu.au).

A strong interest in learners and learning lured **Diana G. Oblinger** away from her academic discipline to information technology. Focusing on ways to enhance learning through information technology, Dr Oblinger has worked in academia, business, and the non-profit sector. Her background as a faculty member and university administrator, along with a commitment to involving students, has given her work a forward-thinking, yet practical tone. Known for her leadership in teaching and learning with technology, she has testified before the US Senate and House committees on technology in higher education and serves on several advisory boards. She is editor or co-editor of seven books and the author or co-author of dozens of monographs and articles as well as a frequent keynote speaker (see www.educause.edu).

In **Barbara Spronk**'s two decades at Athabasca University (1975–96), she had a chance to try almost everything, including tutoring, course authoring, course team supervision and training, International Liaison Officer, project management, and institutional management (Head of Social Sciences, Director of Regional and Tutorial Services, and two acting jobs – Academic Vice-President and Dean of Arts and Science). She earned her Ph.D. in anthropology from the University of Alberta in 1982, and served on the Board of the Canadian Association for Distance Education for ten years, one of those as President. In 1996 she moved to the UK to head up the International Extension College, and worked on projects in over a dozen developing countries. She is now semi-retired in Waterloo, Ontario, happily tutoring online courses.

The interviewees

Had he remained in his native Scotland, **Dominique Abrioux** might have been an excellent candidate to earn a first degree from The Open University (but he settled for an honorary degree from them in 2003). Instead, he emigrated to Canada and finished a traditional university education. Then he joined Athabasca University and stayed for almost three decades, launching Canada's first distance-delivered French language programme and holding increasingly senior positions. As President of Athabasca University (1995–2005), he led its great growth and transformation. Now, notably as Founding President of the Canadian Virtual University/Université canadienne virtuelle Consortium and as a Vice-president of the International Council for Open and Distance Education, he promotes international distance education objectives.

Tony Bates was Director of Distance Education and Technology at the University of British Columbia from 1995 to 2003. He was a founding staff member of the UK Open University where he worked for 20 years. The latest of his eight books is *Technology, e-Learning and Distance Education.* He runs Tony Bates Associates Ltd, specializing in planning and managing e-learning and distance education as a way of ignoring the inevitability of death after retirement. This also helps pay the rent. His real interests, though, are his family (including four grandchildren), skiing, football, golf and flying.

Uli Bernath missed most of first grade when his mother fled with her two boys from East to West at that time in the divided Germany. This turmoil had a lasting impact on his grades in school and his thinking about grades in life. He got to know himself better in sports and grew up as a sportsman rather than a student. His decathlon experiences became meaningful for his whole professional life, which began in 1970 as an assistant professor in economics and will end as the Director of the Center for Distance Education at Carl von Ossietzky University of Oldenburg after exercising that particular metaphorical decathlon for 28 years.

To teach nurses to put patients first became the dream of **Shona Butterfield** after a prolonged period of hospitalization in her teens. At age 33, it became reality as she led the creation of a new nursing school in New Zealand. A 'second chance' distance learner at university, she (much) later became President of The Open Polytechnic of New Zealand where she tried to ensure that all staff innovatively integrated their work to put learners and their needs first. It was a constant challenge when everyone had different ideas about what was best for the student – and government policy didn't always help! Getting an 'evidence base' became increasingly important for developing institutional systems and influencing government policy.

Ronnie Carr was a history teacher and a college of education lecturer before joining the Open University in Scotland as a Staff Tutor in Education in 1976. This post greatly expanded his geographical horizons – not only in the UK but internationally. A secondment to Allama Iqbal Open University in Pakistan was followed by visits/consultancies to a wide range of Asian countries – culminating in his becoming Dean of the School of Education at the Open Learning Institute (subsequently University) of Hong Kong in 1994 – a post he held until 2005. While still an ardent follower of sport – he was the only staff member to play for the Open University rugby team – his workouts are now confined to occasional disco dancing.

Maggie Coats has a passion for both learning and teaching. After training college, she taught in a girls' school in London and then became a student with the new Open University. Six years later she started to tutor for the Open University, alongside other part-time teaching, mainly in women's studies, while she worked towards her Ph.D. at Loughborough University. In 1988 she joined the staff of the Open University at the main campus in Milton Keynes, working with enthusiastic central and regional colleagues on various staff development initiatives. More recently she has faced exciting curriculum development challenges as the university moves towards an outcomes-based approach. The learning and the teaching continue!

In 2003, Graham Gibbs described to an international conference the difficulty of redirecting the ponderous bulk of the supertanker of higher education. He instanced **John Cowan**, pulling sideways from his canoe and – despite his energetic and enthusiastic efforts – having little impact on the juggernaut. John laughed with the others. Yet, subsequently, he has been heartened to note how often prominent teachers, here or abroad, acknowledge that they and their colleagues have made radical changes in their students' learning experiences – as a result of something he said or suggested or did, while he was working with them. He's never seen himself as a leader; he hopes to have been a charismatic catalyst for change.

Immediately after graduating from nursing, **Gail Crawford** married and joined her husband in various academic pursuits. After 10 years and with two children born in Toronto, she moved to join Athabasca University at its inception. For 30 years she held a variety of positions, pioneering the instructional design of nursing and other programmes and generally participating in the exciting, exasperating and fundamentally intriguing development of the university. Despite being officially retired from her faculty position in 2003, she continues teaching in the MDE programme and enjoys working with graduate students from her home. Indeed, she and her husband Doug, also an Athabasca University instructor, toast them in café latte from the deck of their indoor swimming pool!

Raj Dhanarajan grew up in a rubber plantation, in colonial Malaya. Deprivations of all kinds surrounded his childhood and youth, with the most severe being the absence of adequate learning opportunities. It was therefore no surprise when he became seriously attracted to open and distance learning as a way to reach those who ceased to exist in the eyes of elitist campuses. When given an opportunity to help promote learning among those denied it, using innovative distance education models, he grabbed it with both hands. That was 30 years ago. He is still innovating, even following his recent presidency of the Commonwealth of Learning and his earlier leadership of other institutions.

Tony Dodds retired in 2001 as Director of the Centre for External Studies of the University of Namibia where he had been since 1996. He now does occasional consultancy work on open and distance learning for development. Before going to Namibia, he was for 25 years Director of the International Extension College in Cambridge, UK. During that time he helped to set up the Mauritius College of the Air and the Correspondence and Open Studies Unit of the University of Lagos in Nigeria, and helped to develop the University of London Institute of Education's distance education training programmes. In spite of these university posts, his main interest remains in adult basic and non-formal education and how open and distance learning can contribute to this. His other interests include the organization and management of, and professional training in open and distance learning. He has written many articles and contributed to several books on these topics. Most of his working life has been in and about adult education in Africa.

Judith Fage worked for the UK Open University for 26 years. After a career in broadcasting as a studio manager and producer with the BBC, she began teaching part-time for the Open University in 1977. She was inspired by her remarkable students to the realization that this was where she wanted to make her lifetime career, and became a full-time senior counsellor in 1982, part of a team responsible for student support and guidance in the Open University's London Region. In 1997 she became Regional Director and retired in 2004. She has researched and published in the area of student support with a particular interest in career guidance and the development of new technologies for student support and guidance.

Karlene Faith was the director of distance education for the School of Criminology at Simon Fraser University in British Columbia, where she is now Professor Emerita. She is an internationalist and long-time activist for social justice. In 1954, as a 16-year-old stenographer in Saskatchewan, she enrolled in her first college course, by correspondence from the University of Chicago. She raised four children, worked in Europe and East Africa, and in 1981 she received her Ph.D. in the 'History of Consciousness' from the University of California at Santa Cruz. She has taught and published widely in various disciplines, and has authored or co-authored several distance education courses.

When **Glen Farrell** was the President of the Open Learning Agency he would sometimes be asked by younger people interested in 'getting into' distance education what he had studied in order to have a job like that. They were always a bit nonplussed when he told them that his undergraduate degree was in animal science and that it had been a marvellous foundation for a career in education. It was a journey full of twists and turns, mostly unplanned and influenced by opportunity and a few remarkable individuals. And while judging a cattle show in Saskatchewan is quite removed from the policies and applications of learning technologies, it all seemed rather seamless during the journey.

Judith George began unconventionally in her education. As the only girl in the sixth form at an all boys grammar school, she made an appearance on the front page of the *News of the World* for being the only pupil to win a State Scholarship that year. She briefly taught at St Andrews, but got sidetracked again into the alternative university – the Open University. Her passions – technologies in learning, remote learners, action research, access for the very disadvantaged – have always been a little off the mainstream, a tendency she is continuing in retirement with research to rehabilitate the Vandals as devotees of culture – good guys, really!

Chère Gibson failed her first and only distance education course in 1965, an event that tarnished her forever. Lacking the confidence to pursue other distance education and training as a learner, she continues to teach others through a variety of technologies. As a retired faculty member from the University of Wisconsin-Madison, she remains committed to helping others follow a more successful path in distance learning experiences. Her teaching, research and outreach continue to focus on distance education with an emphasis on learner support. Even teaching 'Network Skills for Remote Learning' to engineers still hasn't helped her gain the needed confidence to jump back in to distance learning, however.

Terry Gibson's father was an educator who was an early advocate for the use of technology to improve education. Terry pursued his father's vocation and became intrigued with the potential of technology to reach learners at a distance. During his college years he worked with instructional television and realized that there was more to distance education than just putting a classroom on television. In his graduate education he sought to better understand the design of instruction for distance education in undergraduate, graduate, and continuing education contexts. Throughout his career in the USA in higher education he has worked as instructional designer, teacher, administrator and scholar to improve the quality of distance education.

Dan Granger began hiking when he first started in distance learning in the late 1970s. Working at Empire State College, he hiked all the high peaks of New York's Adirondack Mountains while pondering the many distances to be crossed for learners. In Minnesota he found mountains north of Lake Superior to hike and explore, and in California there were steep and difficult mountains in almost every direction. On retiring from California State University, Dan moved to the Sonoran Desert outside Tucson, Arizona. There, close to grandchildren, he continues learning and crossing distances as a desert naturalist and hiking guide.

Patrick Guiton was a foundation undergraduate at the University of York (UK), a foundation lecturer at the University of Stirling and foundation Director of External Studies at Murdoch University, Western Australia. Immediately before coming to Australia he was a Deputy Regional Director at the Open University. More recently he was an education specialist at the Commonwealth of Learning. Experience in central Africa, rural Scotland and Australia prompted Patrick's interest in the educational and support needs of isolated and itinerant students. He lives in Western Australia, where he teaches English to migrants and refugees; a learning experience that adds a whole new dimension to his understanding of personal, social and educational isolation.

Until he retired from the UK Open University, **Keith Harry** was fortunate enough to travel the world collecting information on distance education and promoting the work and databases of the International Centre for Distance Learning. The pedantic passion for detail which led him to qualify as a librarian and to write a doctoral thesis on the editing of Scottish traditional ballads has subsequently been redirected into co-editing a history of the English village of Grafton Regis, Northamptonshire, where he lives, following the fortunes of his home-town Swindon Town Football Club, and growing well-ordered vegetables in his village allotment.

Before he joined the Open University in 1970, **David Hawkridge** taught teenage boys and co-authored the first geography text of Central Africa; with a Ph.D. from London University on slow-learning children, he trained teachers for African secondary schools. In the USA he evaluated for the US government numerous educational projects for disadvantaged children. At the Open University, he established and led the Institute of Educational Technology for 18 years, then led the development and launching of the Institute's worldwide web-based Masters in Open and Distance Education. His 'take' on distance learning has always been mission-oriented and international. For him, distance learning is about providing learners with opportunities they wouldn't have otherwise had, wherever possible in a national or global setting.

Janet Jenkins spent her entire career working in distance education. Her initial experience was with the National Extension College in the UK. From the mid-1970s until her retirement in 2003 she worked in a variety of different settings and in over 50 countries, initially for the International Extension College and then for the Commonwealth of Learning. In 1993, after three years working back in the UK for the Open Learning Foundation, she began an enjoyable period – which continued until her retirement – as an independent international consultant in distance education. She now lives in England's Lake District.

Brian Kenworthy scraped through Grade 11 at a country technical school in rural Australia before graduating from Geelong Teachers College. Much better academic success occurred in the 1960s and 1970s when he studied education and instructional technology at universities in Canada and the USA, and conducted various action research projects. Since the early 1980s he has designed and evaluated the use of communication and educational technologies for distance education activities aimed at technical and vocational education and university programmes. Notwithstanding his retirement from the University of South Australia in 2003, he has managed consultancies in Vietnam and Papua New Guinea.

Mike Lambert became a true believer in distance learning in the early 1970s, when he saw how his designs for US Army correspondence courses affected the lives of thousands of soldiers around the world. Realizing such educational power, he went to work for the only American accrediting association devoted to educational institutions teaching by correspondence, the National Home Study Council (NHSC). He became Executive Director in 1992, and oversaw the transformation of NHSC into today's Distance Education and Training Council (DETC). Being a frequent traveller for his distance education work (paradoxically) reinforces his conviction that distance education is for the strong of heart and mind.

Playing with an epidiascope as a child and later designing educational materials at the Institute of Army Education (UK) gave **Colin Latchem** a lifelong interest in educational technology. His work in teacher education (UK), academic staff development (Australia) consulting (Africa, India, the Caribbean, China and the South Pacific) and as President of the Open and Distance Learning Association of Australia has prompted many questions about educational change. Since retiring as Head of the Teaching Learning Group at Curtin University in Perth, Australia, he has been a visiting professor/researcher in various leading international post-secondary education and aid agencies. Colin still writes books and articles and teaches online for Athabasca University and the World Health Organization. He'll quit when he's found all the answers to his questions.

Fred Lockwood is now Emeritus Professor of Learning and Teaching, Manchester Metropolitan University, after taking early retirement. A former schoolteacher who trained secondary-school teachers. An educational researcher who taught research methods. A young thing who joined the Open University in the early 1970s and who, over 35 years on, still delights in working with colleagues on the design, production, presentation and evaluation of self-instructional materials. A prolific conductor of seminars and workshops in distance education. An academic who has enabled dozens of colleagues to publish their books and hundreds to publish their articles and book chapters. A catalyst who takes a fairly small part in the reaction but who helps make it work.

Claire Matthewson has worked in distance learning since 1984, when her first job (at the University of Otago) was half-time, temporary and paid from the Equipment Fund. She later became Director of University Extension at The University of the South Pacific, International Programme Director in the Distance Education Centre at Simon Fraser University, and Executive Director, Faculty, at The Open Polytechnic of New Zealand. For family reasons, Claire returned to Otago, 20 years on, and is now the Director, Summer School, and the Adviser, Distance Learning and Continuing Education. The distance learning role is quite small but, for historical reasons as well as continuing challenges, she regards it as a hugely precious part of her current contract.

It was as a kid on the farm lying on the ground and starring up at the night sky filled with so many billions of stars that started **Don McDonell** wondering about things. It was teaching high school that made the concept of education come to life. And it was during his studies in philosophy in Europe that he refined his belief in the power of the instruments used in the manipulation of ideas. It was while teaching philosophy by audio-conferencing in the off-campus centres at the University of Ottawa that he saw the importance of distance education as a means of helping more people discover the world of ideas.

Naomi (Sargant) McIntosh read sociology in the 1950s, thinking she wanted to be a social worker. Being too young for its training, she worked in market research and the Gallup Poll. Twelve years and three children later, she taught marketing/research and created a new part-time degree in public administration. Attracted by the Open University, she set up its Survey Research Department, among many other things. Using research to defend the students (consumers) of the Open University saw her gaining a personal chair and becoming the first Open University female Pro-Vice-Chancellor. She helped establish Channel 4 television (UK), the Open College and the Open Polytechnic. She remained preoccupied with using the media to increase access to educational opportunities rather than allowing new technologies to increase the learning divide. Sadly, Naomi died on July 23, 2006.

Gary Miller started his career in public broadcasting. He discovered distance education when he saw universities innovating with the use of satellite and cable television. A first-generation university graduate who earned two graduate degrees as an adult learner, he understands first-hand how education changes lives and how distance education gives access to those most in need. For more than 35 years his work has been focused at two public universities that have pioneered in adult and distance education – The Pennsylvania State University (where he began and where he currently works) and the University of Maryland University College (where he headed the International University Consortium).

Roger Mills played too much cricket when young and it was only after failing school examinations and being taught by a very enthusiastic biology teacher that he realized that there was more to life than sport. After leaving university he taught in Stratford-on-Avon and then spent five years in teacher education in Liverpool. He moved to Manchester as an Open University science tutor and summer school tutor. There was no looking back; the quality of the teaching and of the students was on a different plane to that which he had experienced before. He joined the Open University in 1971 and stayed until 2004, undertaking a range of roles: senior counsellor, two regional director-ships and Pro-Vice Chancellor.

Louise Moran fell into university life by accident but spent 25 mostly very happy, challenging years making things happen in Australian universities in various capacities as a distance educator, academic administrator and continuing educator. She played an instrumental role in developing Deakin University as a major distance teaching university, and by the time she finished her university career in 1997 had become a (youthful) grand old lady of Australian distance education. After that, she ran a consulting company advising others who make things happen, especially in national policy areas like transnational education and flexible learning. Louise still delights in pushing the boundaries of structures for learning and has an abiding commitment to helping adults stretch their intellectual wings, but from late 2005 on she has been more preoccupied with gardening, social history and writing cookery books.

Ros Morpeth thought she was turning her back on a business career when she embarked on a degree in social anthropology as a mature student. Studying for that degree gave her direct experience of how learning can open a mind and transform a life. On leaving university, Ros fell by chance into a job at the National Extension College (NEC) as a course editor. Immediately feeling 'at home', she stayed with the NEC for 26 years. After directing course development, production and marketing for 10 years, she became the Executive Director (16 years), overseeing a period of dramatic change 'in education demands and how NEC responded across Europe/the United Kingdom'. The business management experience she thought she had left behind proved particularly valuable.

Ian Mugridge came to distance education via his academic discipline of history. He spent several years in teaching and administrative positions at Simon Fraser University in British Columbia and then, in the words of the great Steve McQueen, 'it seemed like a good idea at the time' to accept an offer to set up the degree programme at the new Open Learning Institute (OLI) of British Columbia. This in turn led to 20 years in posts at OLI, its successor, the Open Learning Agency, and the Commonwealth of Learning. His initial decision did turn out to be a good idea, especially with his later helping the development of distance institutions in many parts of the world.

Daryl Nation graduated from Monash University in 1967. Inspirational lecturers, intimate seminars and the early stages of 'the student movement' had made him a firm believer in the virtues of the 'campus experience'. Conscripted into teaching at a distance in 1972, he soon discovered that truly educational experiences could transcend space and time. Since then his work has entailed varying combinations of educational design, management, research and teaching. His special interest has been in exploring educational technologies to maximize dialogue among students and teachers. After he retired from Monash, he took up an honorary position that allows him to continue research work and some teaching.

Hilary Perraton read history at Cambridge and went to work on refuse collection at London County Council. Bored with that, he moved to running examinations and then had the good luck of joining imaginative people – Brian Jackson, Michael Young and Peter Laslett – as they were inventing distance education and setting up the National Extension College. Since 1971 he has worked in international education with periods in Botswana and Barbados, the International Extension College and the Commonwealth Secretariat, followed by seven years setting up and running the International Research Foundation for Open Learning. He now splits his time between cultivating a metaphorical garden, research at the Von Hügel Institute, and serving as deputy chair of the Commonwealth Scholarship Commission.

As a child, **Janet Poley** loved the radio, record player and TV and would sit at the Rural Farm Delivery (RFD) mailbox in Nebraska, USA, waiting for magazines and newspapers. While her family's first TV was magic and a window to a larger world, her parents saw education as the route to a better life for their children. In 1975, with 10 years of educational TV experience and Ph.D. in hand, Janet set out to shrink the world through learning delivered via technology. Forty countries, the internet, and 30 years later, and as Chief Executive Officer and President of the American Distance Education Consortium, she is still driven to pursue social justice and learning worldwide.

Gisela Pravda was an established teacher of economics and business administration when she realized that women were being required to adapt to male-oriented education models. Seeing a clear example of sexist course materials in Colombia while there for six years showed her the ways of excluding women students. Gender-related issues in evaluating vocational and post-secondary education in Germany thus became her key interest. Over two decades of lobbying, research, arguments and action projects, she can see some progress; for example, in the adding of gender aspects to the obligatory use of course evaluation criteria. After being pensioned, she earned a Ph.D. in education and gender studies and founded a small consultancy on gender issues.

Tom Prebble served as Director of Extramural Studies and later Principal of Extramural and International Studies at Massey University in New Zealand from 1986 to 2002. These roles placed him at the head of New Zealand's largest dual mode distance education operation as it grew from a student enrolment of some 5000 to over 20,000. He came to that role from an earlier academic career in educational administration, and left it to take up the Chair in Higher Education at Massey. He is currently engaged in consulting work in international education and quality assurance. During his time in distance education, Tom served as President of the Distance Education Association of New Zealand and participated in a range of international conferences, workshops and consultancies in the field.

Educated in Ecuador, Switzerland and England, **Greville Rumble** joined the Open University. He held various administrative and managerial posts between 1970 and 1998, including two appointments as the university's Corporate Planner and two as a Regional Director. He was appointed Professor of Distance Education Management in 1998 and left the Open University in 2001 to work as a private consultant. His expertise is in the costs, financing and management of distance education (his Ph.D. from the Open University is on the costs and economics of distance education).

'I got the virus' is the most-often used phrase of **Bernd Schachtsiek**, who fell in love with distance learning after he entered the business in 1977. From then on, he promoted various distance learning models, not only in his 'own' institutes that served more than 60,000 students each year in German-speaking countries, from leisure courses to university degrees, but also as President of the German Association for Distance Teaching Institutes (DFV) for 16 years and as President of the European Association for Distance Learning (EADL) for 14 years. He still believes that excellent service and outstanding quality are the keys to success in a market where government-funded education institutions are still the most powerful players.

Lee Taylor was part of the generation of middle-class girls who benefited from the expansion of higher education in the 1960s, and has remained a believer in extending access and confronting inequities since encountering class and racial prejudice in the UK and USA as a teenager. She counts herself lucky to have been involved in the Open University since 1972, with the opportunity to undertake around 20 or so different roles there, including Director of Equal Opportunities and partnership work with the health service. She is committed to increased access to health and education both at a local, UK and (where possible) international level.

John Thomas was educated at Durham and Yale, and started his professional life as a political scientist at Essex University in the mid-1960s. He joined the BBC in 1969 as an educational radio producer, working first on Open University programmes and then in continuing education. He taught radio and educational broadcasting at Christ Church College, Canterbury (1981–86). Since 1983, he has been involved in consultancy and training in the use of radio and audio for distance education, working mainly in Africa under the auspices of the International Extension College. Now retired from full-time work, he lives in London with his partner Anne.

David Warr's professional area was distance education in the third world, especially applied to non-formal and secondary level education, particularly in Central and Southern Africa and Pakistan. This has involved him in course development, training, evaluation, consultancy and a great deal of practical application. Particular interests: working with local staff to set up structures and procedures for distance education that are appropriate, and effective and sustainable practical research to ensure the effectiveness of media and methods. Driving forces: the needs and the willing response of learners in the developing world, the enthusiasm and dedication of fellow practitioners in the field, and the support of colleagues.

J. Colin Yerbury was expelled from high school for defiantly chewing gum in class. Forced to take Grade 12 physics by correspondence, he felt the wonders of academic achievement through independent study. Accepted as a mature student at Simon Fraser University (SFU) shortly after it opened (1965), he graduated four times from it and never left it: hired as SFU's first Director of Distance Education, he became a Professor of Criminology before serving punishment as the third Dean of Continuing Studies. Life-long learning and distance education have driven his professional commitment to learners in Canada and internationally. He thinks of finishing high school, but at a distance where he can chew gum as an emancipated thinker.

Part 1

Introducing the book

1

'Breaking new ground'

Liz Burge

... crafting the future ... pushing boundaries ...

(Shona Butterfield)

[I was] part of something quite extraordinary in education in the late twntieth century.

(Roger Mills)

Introduction

This book honours the lived experience of international pioneers in post-secondary/higher education. These pioneers lived through, in their words, 'exciting' times. They pushed conventional limits to create extraordinary learning opportunities for millions of adults. What they learned then needs explicating now to a wider audience of practitioners and researchers in post-secondary education. This book asks you to consider their learning and assess their transference (or fertilizing) power for your contexts. Technologies for learning come and may go but basic questions and conditions for effective learning persist across the decades.

By 2003, something was happening on the horizons of my professional landscape, and it did not feel good! Some sources of collegiality and inspiration I had experienced for a quarter century were beginning to disappear. A significant generation of leaders in open and flexible forms of higher education either had retired recently or were facing retirement from full-time, paid, institution-based work. Their reputations had been made and maintained variously via publications, practice-based achievements, and thoughtful reflections at conferences. I surely would miss them for their passionately-held values, engaging narratives from practice, and hard-won strategic wisdom. What also made me pause was the additional impending loss to the public realm of their career reflections. I had to do something.

Time to think

Such a loss seemed important for two reasons. First, there was the quality of their experiential knowledge. Some of that knowledge exists in their refereed publications, but such formal knowledge differs from what might be revealed via narratives and reflections generated during in-depth and real-time interviews. Consider, for example, these idiosyncratic statements of personal beliefs that emerged in just three interviews.

> I came away [from the US Army] with the excitement that you can change human lives with [distance education]; and it's not something to be toyed with.
>
> (Michael Lambert)

> . . . in my speeches . . . I'm going to keep distance in distance education as long as we still have learners who are distant. And when we've solved all the distance problems in terms of education and the access issues, then we can drop this thing.
>
> (Janet Poley)

> For me [distance education] is primarily about flexibility and access . . . It is very much around the ability to accommodate the student's particular requirements in terms of start dates, flexibility in terms of the lengths they might need, the length of time they might want to take to do the course, and the fact that they don't have to leave their home or place of work or whatever in order to do the course.
>
> (Ros Morpeth)

A second reason for regretting the loss was the kind of higher education work practised by these pioneers. They have gone boldly into often unmapped and difficult territories to create sustainable and flexible post-secondary educational opportunities for millions of adults unable or unwilling to fit into time- and place-bound classrooms. In the words of Greville Rumble, they were 'changing higher education so that it is more flexible in its attitude to what is permissible'. Passion and commitment sustained their actions:

> In the early years of distance education . . . these pioneers had the courage and determination to work beyond the mainstream: [it] was almost like an evangelical religion. It was driven by people who cared; who had a mission and who wanted to make education an opportunity for all.
>
> (Gail Crawford)

> Professionals in distance education . . . were not accepted by the majorities; . . . in the seventies we were far out there.
>
> (Ulrich Bernath)

Most of the adults needing new educational opportunities lived in cities and towns in financially rich and not-so-rich countries; not in geographically isolated areas as the term 'distance' might imply. The adults lived inside various socioeconomic strata, and not always in the middle layers:

> I remember sitting at the back of an open-air adult literacy tutorial group in a remote village in Pakistan. The people there ranged from young children to the very old. I shared a hookah with an old man while a young Pakistani woman taught English using materials we had developed at Allama Iqbal Open University. For me, this was very moving experience. We were really doing something very practical there.
>
> (Ronnie Carr)

In leading, administering or planning new institutions, in developing engaging, high-quality course materials, training tutors and advisory personnel, choosing appropriate technologies for learning and teaching, and in building innovative partnerships with other providers, the pioneers were driven by the need for demonstrable success, as the literature of the time so clearly indicated. What the literature omitted then, though, were the affective elements, factors in human behaviour that are now recognized as important in understanding the links between emotions-based responses to a context and the subsequent cognitive decisions about appropriate behaviour. 'What we were doing was really important and . . . we had to do it properly; and I think we all found it very exciting. And that helped a lot with the stress' (Ian Mugridge). In opening and keeping open the metaphorical doors to richer lives or new careers for their students, they had to think inclusively and holistically if visible success was to happen:

> There was such a feeling of breaking new ground, of being different and having a very important sort of social and educational integrity . . . it was enabling people to develop and find their own voices . . . What we were remitted to do was to find out ways . . . to enable people who hadn't had a chance or needed a second chance, to come into education. We had to develop the content and the framework of education that would help them to do that, and we also therefore had to look at new ways of supporting them, taking them seriously as learners in a way that was never done in conventional universities. This, for many of our students, meant looking at their affective needs as well as cognitive ones, at building their confidence and attuning them to the culture and values of higher education.
>
> (Judith George)

As change agents in higher education, they worked in fast-moving and very complex, multi-layered contexts. They had to figure out, with a critical mindset, how and where informed change might best succeed, and then stay focused on key values as they moved to implement:

> a really important aspect of leadership, particularly when you're running an institution that is different, is being able to influence the environment in which you operate. So that means not just accepting

the policy environment that you operate in and creating a clear vision within that, but creating a vision that helps influence the government to change their policy.

(Shona Butterfield)

. . . it's all been about the adoption and diffusion of innovation and managing change in educational systems.

(Glen Farrell)

At every level we are seeing the online learning environment really change the way instruction is conducted at the institution. We haven't lost access to the distance student but we've gained all this other stuff; and the blending promises to be a very, very important thing for us. It's exciting.

(Gary Miller)

Would any of today's higher education practitioners want to know about such experience and attitudes? Are today's contexts so different, making irrelevant the recorded experience of the last quarter of the twentieth century? The year 2006 marked the 150th year of institutionally 'organized' distance education (Holmberg 1995). Activity levels in distance modes of post-secondary education now are high, with, for example, virtual modes of university operations gaining attention (D'Antoni 2006). Large numbers of adult students participate. The Open University (UK) (www.open.ac.uk) now manages approximately 200,000 students at undergraduate and postgraduate levels, Canada's Athabasca University (www.athabascau.ca) 32,000 (per year), and the Open University of Hong Kong approximately 20,000 students annually (www.ouhk.edu.hk). In India, the Indira Gandhi National Open University serves 1.4 million students with 125 courses delivered with assistance from 1400 study centres (www.ignou.ac.in/). Working with 53 Commonwealth member countries, the Commonwealth of Learning (www.col.org) facilitates the design and distribution of professional development activities for distance educators and promotes wider access to quality learning for millions of students (at all levels) around the world. On the African continent, the African Virtual University (www.avu.org) works with seven large international universities and six well-established funding partners. In the USA, the Distance Education and Training Council (www.detc.org) accredits approximately 100 distance study institutions, from the elementary, secondary, postsecondary (degree and career) and doctoral levels, serving nearly 4 million students worldwide. Several million adults learn for vocational or other reasons via members of the the European Association for Distance Learning (EADL) (www.eadl.org): privately-funded, non-governmental institutes of training and education. As a non-profit organization the EADL represents over 500 distance learning institutes through 65 members, associated national and international organizations and individuals in about 20 European countries. From being one of three US universities to launch the first ever distance mode courses in 1892, Penn

State University established 106 years later the 'World Campus' which now offers online 50 programmes with 25,400 enrolments to students scattered across 40 countries (www.worldcampus.psu.edu).

The degree of relevance may depend on one's vantage point and values. In this case, the longer one's view of postsecondary education, the greater are the expectations that while some things change, other things do not, at least essentially. The hyperbole regarding emerging technologies, for example, can be judged against that of technological change in earlier generations. The intrapersonal and interpersonal processes of learning carry cognitive and affective demands and impact on learners and teachers in a similar way to that of 150 years ago. The impact of learners' own life contexts and the actual and sustained availability of resources, as the final example, are still the guiding factors in how expert, long-view educators conduct their learning experiences. Consider this narrative about context-sensitive tutoring for a university course:

> My student sat me down at the kitchen table with a mug of coffee, and we waited for her husband to come in from doing the rounds with the mail – he was going to join in the tutorial as well, it appeared. Then her uncle came in from milking the goats to join us. Then their two boys, given a day off school for this purpose, sat down. And finally, the goats themselves wandered in and joined the group. Everyone contributed – Kant was obviously the focus of the family conversation in the croft that week; everyone was wrestling with the moral imperative. And I thought 'YES! This is what education is really about!'
>
> (Judith George)

Postsecondary educators with shorter experiential views of distance and flexible learning may assume that lessons learned 25 years ago are not so relevant for today's contexts. The key technology, they tend to argue (in conversations with me, at least), has changed from correspondence to online and the technology purchase price has become so much lower that access is no longer the issue; new methods of learning and teaching inside technology are the issues. Would everyone agree on that after reading this book? Quality assurance is also a current issue for others, but many decades of practice underlie, for example, the detailed quality standards used by all members of EADL across Europe or the British *Code of Practice for the Assurance of Academic Quality and Standards in Higher Education: Section 2: Collaborative Provision and Flexible and Distributed Learning (including e-learning)* (www.qaa.ac.uk).

Collegial experience and my own learning suggest that some gaps exist in the professional knowledge of some practitioners: they need information on the battles fought about the role and status of alternative forms of postsecondary education, on the lessons learned about the technological mediation of learning by adults, on the conditions necessary for sustainable innovation, or even on the now large body of journal and book literature (for examples of aggregated information, see Moore and Anderson 2003; Evans *et al.* 2007). Some of the pioneers in this study agree (without prompting), stating:

the new time cannot be well understood without the old time. Much of what is good practice in the new time comes from the old times and much of what explains the . . . low standard of what is going on in the new times comes from ignorance with respect to the old times . . . In the late nineties we met a lot of new, fresh faces . . . who thought that the world has started with the web in '95.

(Ulrich Bernath)

. . . it seems if it wasn't published three years ago, it doesn't exist. And that's tragic. I just see so many people in the field, supposedly educational technologists [or] designers, oblivious of the work of others.

(Fred Lockwood)

Relevance may also be based in professional values and institutional conditions. How far do today's competitive educational contexts go in considering and assuring equitable access to education (a canon of 'distance education'), rather than in pursuing income generation from lucrative market segments? How many higher education institutions now can afford to give less experienced teaching staff regular help from people skilled in course design or quality-assurance procedures for teaching (another canon), despite the alleged benefits of using online software templates? How much time can be dedicated to seeking the hard-won experience of 'elders', given the burdens of time-pressed institutional operations and academic output measures?

You will decide for yourself about these relevance arguments. I will discover the relevance for my own practice only after I have 'unearthed' the experiential knowledge of the pioneers and compared it against today's dynamics and my own values and beliefs.

Hence this book. It is a mark of respect to members of a significant generation of higher education pioneers. It synthesizes their individual reflections and narratives. It does not, therefore, focus on the histories of institutions or projects. Narratives help access the personal 'self', which in turn 'gives coherence and continuity to the scramble of experience' (Bruner 2002: 73). Narrative in societies is thus 'serious business' (Bruner 2002: 107). Narrative reveals how the speaker models her or his world and explains (especially unintended) actions and results in ways that maintain a coherent sense of a functioning 'self'. For instance, in Professor Judith George's comments above and Sir John Daniel's in Chapter 8, their narratives act as 'sites where agency is played out' (Denzin 2004: xii). If you accept this idea of agency – how individuals act, construct their own realities, interpret others' constructions of reality and maintain personal effectiveness – then you will gain insights into how postsecondary educators 'accept, negotiate, challenge, or even actively resist the positionings provided for them by dominant discursive forms' (Bradbury and Sclater 2004: 194). In short, this whole book asks you to consider where, why and how experiential wisdom from yesterday may inform your work of today.

While this book appears to be the first of its kind in focusing personally on a particular generation of distance education pioneers, it situates itself with several others using an overtly reflective focus on the experience of distance modes of postsecondary education (Evans and Nation 1989, 1993, 2000; Burge and Haughey 2001; Latchem and Hanna 2001; Kearsley 2005). The journal literature carries a few items too; for example, Burge *et al.* (2000), Cochrane (2000) and Tolley (2000).

Time to act

Finding participants

After discussing the book idea with some colleagues around the world and competing nationally for research funding, I developed an initial invitation list of approximately 25 pioneers who fitted the criteria (comparatively recent or impending retirement from work associated with the education or training of adults, focusing on postsecondary credit programmes). Requests were sent through my networks for discreet suggestions. A reasonable breadth of first language, geographic, institutional and gender representation were additional factors in searching for potential names. A limit of this first list is the predominance of people for whom English is their first language. A future study, with adequate travel and translation/interpretation resources to enable interviewees to use their preferred language, must include recent or soon-to-be retirees from countries in the African continent, Europe, all five Nordic countries, Asia, South-East Asia, and Oceania. Expectedly, not everyone accepted my invitation. Unexpectedly, the final number of actual interviews grew to 46 – almost double the funded estimate. Two interviewees did not return their transcripts, so 44 approved and amended transcripts became the data source, providing approximately 580,000 words for analysis. From here on, interviewees will be known as participants; thus walking my talk about respect for what interviewees give to researchers.

The geography of the experience discussed in the interviews is broad – Canada (8 participants), Germany (3), Hong Kong (1), multiple countries (i.e., international development contexts) (7), Oceania (Australia, New Zealand and South Pacific) (8), UK (11), USA (6). The type of professional experience is categorized broadly as institutional leadership (9), institutional unit/faculty/departmental level administration (12), programme/curricula development/evaluation (6), teaching skill development (5), technology applications (4), research/documentation (3), and development aid in various countries (5). Thirty-four participants worked predominantly with universities or polytechnics offering credit programmes and 5 with government aid agencies. Two participants led mostly self-funded institutions, 2 currently lead consortia organizations, and 1 was a senior staff member in a national government educational evaluation and research office.

Behind such facts lie the personalities. For their biographical statement (designed to model this book's emphasis on the reflective and idiosyncratic 'person' underlying the professional reputation), the participants each chose what they wanted you to know. My request was to add some 'colour' indicative of their personality, values, or life events and to avoid the typical chronological *curriculum vitae* summary. More details of some of their published professional contributions nest in Part 5.

Collecting data

Each participant received the interview protocol well ahead of time. It prompted them to reflect on their practice by exploring a range of topics: key challenges faced, guiding ideas, values, etc., for their practice; stressors experienced, lessons learned, technology managed; career highlights and lowlights; perceptions on any significant changes in distance education during their career; and factors that sustained their careers. Looking forward, they opined about possible research projects, offered any suggestions they had for younger or less experienced colleagues, and identified concerns for the future of distance and/or higher education.

Developing these major areas for data-gathering took time and forced me to face my own meaning-making about my career: 'How might I best respond to such an interview? What does it mean to interrogate my own career? How might I be led past self-enhancing stories, chronologies or plain factual descriptions?' Taking such a 'constructivist' approach means respecting and encouraging a person's capacity for meaning-making and looking for their 'assumptions, implicit meanings, and tacit rules' (Charmaz 2006: 32). It took even more time to finalize the forms of the questions. Key guidelines were to keep questions short in words but long in opportunity, not leading the participant with biasing questions, not asking either too vague or unduly complex questions, restricting my spoken reactions to facilitative comments and valuing the thinking silences.

Most interviews took between two and two and a half hours, either in face-to-face or audio-conferenced (AC) mode (my 20+ years of AC for graduate teaching helped.) Probes to encourage, elaborate, signal my acute attention, clarify, steer the 'conversation' and look for sequences and evidence (Rubin and Rubin 2005: 164–72), with some paraphrasing, enabled me to gain more depth and breadth and confirm or correct what I had just heard. Institutional histories were not the focus, so some steering was needed at times. Each interviewee used their own combination of narratives, types of thinking, anecdotes, metaphors, spontaneous reflections, pauses and puzzlements to keep my brain running at very high speed. Not every participant answered every question directly or in the original sequence, but no participant left the interview indicating that she or he wanted to say more. Thoughtful preparation was evident. Many commented that the exercise had helped them reflect in new ways; for example, in helping them recall or synthesize. I left each interview feeling privileged, challenged to rethink some of my own experience, and reconnected to aspects of 'something quite extraordinary' (Roger Mills) in postsecondary education.

Analysing the data

The qualitative data analysis involved two major stages. The first stage was the selection and aggregation, from within individual transcripts and across all 44 transcripts, of all pertinent comments related to each major topic. As expected from the way most people recall and recount experience, many participants approached their reflections via some sideways narratives, multiple beginnings or revisits to a topic question. The aggregation and winnowing process resulted in files of quite varied sizes: for example, the 'challenges' file held (approximately) 85,000 words; 'lessons learned' 63,000; 'guides to practice' 57,000; 'technology' 42,000; and 'significant changes' 19,000.

The second stage reduced the file contents to more synthesized meanings. During this period I kept asking: 'Which are the important recollections from each participant's perspective? What is the range of experience to be represented? Which transcript extracts will best support my analyses? How do I ensure that their voices, not mine, predominate? Given the word limits for this book, is there room for enough rich detail for the commentators and readers?' Time was needed for developing and revising code categories, reducing detail, writing analytical memos, rechecking what should be brought together against evidence in the transcripts, and synthesizing to a level where adequate representation had emerged. The process was iterative and recursive too – cycles of coming into very close focus with the data and then stepping backwards to gain a broader perspective and 'fresh eyes' for a revisit. The use of quotations is a deliberate strategy (not an abdication of synthetic thinking), to foreground individual voices and add nuance and colour.

Space for meta-reflections

Commentaries by seven well-known experts provide a meta-level of reflection (Part 3). All commentators but one still work full-time. Each one brings high levels of expertise in either postsecondary/higher education generally or distance education specifically, as well as a willingness to think critically and creatively. Each is guided by his or her experiential wisdom and my request to make explicit the salient links they detect between the lessons of past expert practice and the demands of current contexts. How 'salience' is defined is each commentator's choice. Several guiding questions were offered to each commentator: 'How do you react to what you've read in some or all of the findings chapters? Where are the highlights for you? Where are the puzzles and surprises, if any? What is in the reported experience (1) that today's younger or less experienced practitioners and researchers might consider, and (2) that might promote theory-building or practice enhancement for postsecondary education?'

It is time now to immerse yourself in the pioneers' realities and the commentators' reactions. Seek some peaceful time to reflect. Consider which discourses, values, expectations and goals dominate your work world, and how far the pioneers' reflections and values link to that world. Enjoy the journey.

References

Bradbury, P. and Sclater, S.D. (2004) Conclusion, in M. Andrews, S.D. Sclater, C. Squire and A. Treacher (eds) *The Uses of Narrative: Explorations in Sociology, Psychology and Cultural Studies*. Somerset, NJ: Transaction Publishers.

Bruner, J. (2002) *Making Stories: Law, Literature, Life*. New York: Farrar, Straus & Giroux.

Burge, E.J. and Haughey, M. (eds) (2001) *Using Learning Technologies: International Perspectives on Practice*. London: RoutledgeFalmer.

Burge, E.J., Laroque, D. and Boak, C. (2000) Baring professional souls: reflections on web life, *Journal of Distance Education*, 15(1): 81–98.

Charmaz, K. (2006) *Constructing Grounded Theory: A Practical Guide Through Qualitative Analysis*. London: Sage.

Cochrane, C. (2000) Reflections of a distance learner 1977–1997, *Open Learning*, 15(1): 17–34.

D'Antoni, S. (ed.) (2006) *The Virtual University: Models and Messages; Lessons from Case Studies*. Paris: UNESCO, http://publishing.unesco.org/details.aspx?Code_Livre=4478 (accessed 30 November 2006).

Denzin, N. (2004) Foreword, in M. Andrews, S.D. Sclater, C. Squire and A. Treacher (eds) *The Uses of Narrative: Explorations in Sociology, Psychology and Cultural Studies*. Somerset, NJ: Transaction Publishers.

Evans, T., Haughey, M. and Murphy, D. (eds) (2007) *The World Handbook of Distance Education*. London: Elsevier.

Evans, T. and Nation, D. (eds) (1989) *Critical Reflections on Distance Education*. London: Falmer Press.

Evans, T. and Nation, D. (eds) (1993) *Reforming Open and Distance Education*. London: Kogan Page.

Evans, T. and Nation, D. (eds) (2000) *Changing University Teaching: Reflections on Creating Educational Technologies*. London: Kogan Page.

Holmberg, B. (1995) The evolution of the character and practice of distance education, *Open Learning*, 10(2): 47–52.

Kearsley, G. (2005) *Online Learning: Personal Reflections on the Transformation of Education*. Englewood Cliffs, NJ: Educational Technology Publications.

Latchem, C. and Hanna, D. (eds) (2001) *Leadership for 21st Century Learning*. London: Kogan Page.

Moore, M.G. and Anderson, W. G. (eds) (2003) *Handbook of Distance Education*. Mahwah, NJ: Erlbaum.

Rubin, H.J. and Rubin, I. S. (2005) *Qualitative Interviewing: The Art of Hearing Data*, 2nd edn. Thousand Oaks, CA: Sage.

Tolley, S. (2000) How electronic conferencing affects the way we teach, *Open Learning*, 15(3): 253–65.

Part 2

The pioneers reflect

2

Facing challenges: 'no prior experience', quality, and management

Liz Burge

Institutional management, course design and production, learner needs, and having 'no prior experience to draw on' (Greville Rumble) emerged as the largest organizing categories for the participants' challenges. These are reported here. Other areas of challenge, such as faculty resistance to distance mode teaching (a sometimes covert issue but always delicate to handle), funding (often in doubt or deficit) and technology use are mentioned here and discussed in more detail in other chapters. The challenge of reputation has its own paragraph at the end, because this challenge was often mentioned.

You will not see the solutions to the challenges here; first, because they were not part of the key focus of the study; and second, if solutions had begun to emerge, collecting and analysing all that information would have required more resources than were available within project constraints.

Before heading into the institutional management category, the 'no prior experience' category needs illumination because it was experienced and recalled as a pervasive condition of professional life.

'No prior experience'

The phrase means much more than needing to learn new skills for established jobs. The jobs themselves had to be designed *in situ*. Hilary Perraton pointed out, while discussing his planning and training work with the National Extension College in the UK in the mid-1960s, that 'distance education didn't exist; we had to invent it'. Elsewhere in the UK, at the new Open University (OUUK), the earliest researchers in the application of technology to adults' learning were, as Tony Bates, explained, 'blundering around in the dark'. While educational broadcasting had attracted some research by the British Broadcasting Corporation (BBC), it had not gained the attention of educators. So Tony and his educational media research colleagues faced 'a completely new area, and I had nothing to really fall back on. I had no methodologies or theories to really guide the research ... It took [us] a while to work it out.' One of his colleagues, already highly experienced in social survey research across the UK and known for her skill in 'understanding what people want', worked on the design of a student registration form for the OUUK that eventually would facilitate UK-wide student monitoring and demographic analyses. Naomi (Sargant) McIntosh and her colleagues lacked external guidance for such design work: '... this wasn't out of anybody's theory or textbook; this was out of my head and our heads and our discussions and practical common sense'. Later she found herself again in a challenging innovation with no templates, this time in the establishment of the Channel 4 television station in the UK, designed to reach a much larger and wider population base than that attracted to the OUUK. Its mandate was to design programmes to illustrate how people might enrich their lives culturally and educationally. With no TV experience, and trade critics publicly reflecting on that skill deficit, she found the challenge to be, initially, 'absolutely scary'.

On the other side of the Atlantic, somewhat later, similar ground-up efforts were being designed. One Canadian and one US interviewee mentioned their lack of experience in distance education institutional and technological innovations, but such 'innocence' did not deter their efforts. As Ian Mugridge rapidly set up the degree programme of the then Open Learning Institute, he used his best guesses and prior networks from his professorial life in a traditional university:

> there were no models that seemed to us to be appropriate. And so the structure that we used internally and the way we organized ourselves was really making it up as we went along. We had to; it was to a very large extent our best guess.

Glen Farrell commented on the lack of a research base that, in his early work as the President and Chief Executive Officer of the Open Learning Agency in British Columbia, forced him and his colleagues to develop their own context-appropriate mixed-method course delivery models. Gary Miller, later still in the mid-1990s, in helping to set up Penn State University's internet-based World Campus, felt a kind of *déjà vu* as he compared the work of his current colleagues to his own work two decades earlier in using technology linkages to aggregate students and programmes: '[World Campus colleagues] are the ones who are doing in this environment what I was doing back in the seventies. They were inventing, and I remember they didn't have any rules to play by in the beginning either.'

The sharp edges of 'no prior experience' showed up in some other aspects. One was market potential and thus having to plan for and design self-administered questionnaires and application forms for large-scale distribution. Here Naomi (Sargant) McIntosh and colleagues faced 'fundamental' issues and procedural questions, since so much was at stake in building a successful and credible OUUK and silencing the noisy public critics:

What did you put on the first application form? What did you ask people about if it was really going to be open and be seen to be open? . . . How did you persuade people that this university was really open, that 'you weren't going to be interviewed, that you weren't going to be required to have qualifications'? How did you do that? How did you know enough about the people who were coming in order to be able to make a judgement about whether they could access the study centres, whether they would need help? How could you build in any sort of prior indicators? . . . nobody had done anything like this before.

Another site of newness in the OUUK was institutional development. Greville Rumble recalled seven challenges in his work: the accelerated development of courses to meet an acceleration of the timing of the first student intake (in early 1971); the design of an integrated student records management system; the establishment of the student tuition and counselling system; and the 'defining roles' of the various types of learner-assisting staff, academic productivity, forecasting student numbers, and resource allocation across the institution. For example, his efforts to integrate the academic staff with the materials production staff in order to ensure very high-quality course materials with cost-effective output shows how he and others had to face new but critically important questions:

> What was the role of an editor? What happened when stuff came back at page proof and the academics reread them and made lots of changes and the editor wanted to pass all the academics' changes, which sent the budget sky-high? Were there any constraints? How did we deal with academics who handed over manuscripts late and jeopardized the printing schedules or even the availability of the materials at the start of the course? Were there any sanctions that could be applied? How were we going to print all this material? Were we going to have an in-house printing industry or were we going to have a limited in-house capability and put most of it out to X-number of printers? What about copyright? How much copyrighted material could be included? What if we were selling materials outside areas covered by the copyright agreements we had? What about the TV and radio? How did that integrate with the texts?

Despite his planner's analytical mind and the existence of some related but external sources of help, he was not above admitting that having 'no prior experience to draw on' did sometimes force improvisations and occasional bold guesses, even some that used the age-old method of 'licking your finger, sticking it into the air, and coming up with a figure'. As with other colleagues in this study, he also experienced great mental stimulation: '. . . there was nothing that said how you plan a distance teaching university . . . So we were . . . pioneering – it was intellectually challenging, interesting work. Fascinating.' Chère Gibson's reflections at times showed an innovator's confidence toward a political challenge. Here she recalls her artfulness at the University of Wisconsin-Madison in both protecting scarce new project funding and demanding full accountability to ensure its intended use: 'So I [was economical with the truth] and told them that those were special line items funding from the Legislature and they need to monitor it in a special line so we could account for every penny! And it worked. Let them think you know what you are talking about!'

A further domain of *de novo* innovation was research. Tony Dodds's recollection of early days at the International Extension College pointed to the lack of published prior knowledge, either theoretical or practical. No refereed journal articles or books yet existed to help his inductive and deductive reasoning about his practice: '. . . we lived through the development of the theories of distance education and distance learning. I don't think anyone had thought about a theory of distance education when we started.' Tony Bates, while at the OUUK in its early years, faced a problem of interpreting his broadcasting research data: how to interpret the results in a perceived intellectual vacuum? 'The methodology wasn't the problem. The problem was, what do I make of the results when I have got them and how do I interpret the results? . . . we made it up as we went, I am afraid, because there wasn't much else that we could do.'

Supporting knowledge development was the documentation of emerging field activity and its reporting literature – the fugitive, 'grey' material as well as the more accessible refereed journals. Keith Harry took leadership in this infrastructure area. For over 25 years, before web-based databases had been invented, he led international efforts to create and computerize databases for practitioners, policy-makers and researchers. Keith's work in the International Centre for Distance Learning, based at the OUUK, was the first of its kind: 'By the end of eighties we were getting quite a lot of visitors and people coming along who were using the library and . . . also using the databases.' Later they built a database of courses, in association with the Commonwealth of Learning.

To summarize this section, consider Janet Jenkins's reflections as a consultant helping governments and educational institutions in many countries plan the implementation of distance mode learning. Here she refers to discussions with senior administrators at a prominent and large-scale single-mode (i.e. exclusively distance mode) university in South-East Asia: 'They would argue about anything, and that was quite fun, but it could be quite frightening because you really were on the edge of your knowledge all the time.' Years before, in her work with the National Extension College, experimenting with what mixes of learning materials best fitted with which learners' needs, she knew what the 'edge' felt like:

> Really nobody had a clue about what you should do to develop the materials. There was some notion of learning objectives, and that trying to make materials interactive might be a good idea. We developed these ideas on the hoof, you know; just from trying things and seeing what worked – trying them out with teachers or whoever was the target group

and seeing if they liked them and working from there. So that was really very exciting.

Institutional management

Many participants reported their challenges as a complex mix of managing institutional change and improving the efficiency of educational service delivery. The institutions or operations mentioned below are treated in sequence to enable a focus on each one. Let us take New Zealand first.

Tom Prebble led distance education service activities for 14 years in the dual-mode (face-to-face classroom and distance teaching) Massey University. Guided by wanting to avoid 'an oppressive sort of management, or an industrial culture' in his operation, he saw his initial challenge as sustaining attention to all the logistical services needed by academics and learners:

> I was keen that the extramural function should continue to serve the interests of teachers and students, and not drive them; the train should run on time. That the study material would be produced in a timely fashion, that assignments would flow in and out of the place effectively and that feedback to students was speedy.

While academics in their faculties were creating and preparing course content and learning assessments for distance mode (extramural) students, Tom insisted on maintaining the equivalence and status of the degrees being offered in distance mode. Many academics designed their course materials for double use and double benefit: 'we tend to use the lessons of the extramural mode to inform our internal teaching, so the great majority of internal courses use extramural study material as well'. 'Quality assurance screens' had to operate; for example, providing very advanced notice of a new course to be developed and well-publicized work performance indicators that would act also to build confidence from senior university administrators. Here is one example of a screen:

> All 100,000 assignments were coming in to one office, being dispersed to markers, and then being gathered back, by the unit, and repackaged up. So, we had a standard that everything had to go through the house in 24 hours to have a simple standard to have to meet, and on a sort of no-excuses basis. You just had to do it.

High levels of operational efficiency in his distance unit served well the challenge of keeping distance mode operations highly respected, academically and operationally, around the university: '. . . one of the risks of a dual-mode institution is that the extramural operation either becomes a Cinderella or just sort of drops out of sight. And other priorities tend to push it aside from time to time.' So Tom made it his business to explain to Massey's Vice Chancellor that his distance unit carried societal and institutional significance, shown, for example, in statistics: 'a third of our business, a third of our income . . . 20,000 New Zealanders out there studying. We've got to look after them.'

Very soon after joining the now-named Open Polytechnic of New Zealand – He Wharekura-tini Kaihautu o Aotearoa (OPNZ) – as its Chief Executive, Shona Butterfield confronted various threats to its ongoing operations. Taking on the 'fight to survive' in the public realm and looking to gain more power for negotiating site agreements for OPNZ service provision, she began the difficult internal process of generating institutional attitudes, skill sets, policies and procedures needed for coherence in learning and teaching service delivery and effective institutional management. Finding out how many students actually were registered in the OPNZ and changing the ratio of teaching to administrative staff to gain greater operational efficiency were just two subsidiary challenges in this institutional renewal process. During her first year as Chief Executive the major challenge sharpened dramatically:

> . . . suddenly we had a budget of 30 something million dollars from the [earlier] 1.8 and we were expected to manage our own institution. We had no human resources; we had no marketing department; we had no finance department, or any IT infrastructure to do this. So my first year was absolutely just restructuring the organization to have it able to even survive and then begin to build where I'd go for the future.

Not long after the rebuilding processes began, more challenges arrived – this time external ones in the form of government policy changes regarding industry training (leading to 'significant redundancies' in OPNZ staffing), funding cutbacks and the imposition of student fees. Internal ongoing difficulties arose from differences of opinion and values between levels of staff:

> *Liz:*   . . . the key [learner service] staff were not in leadership posi-
> tions, so they were being controlled or supervised by people
> who did not have the same vision that the staff members agreed
> with?
>
> *Shona:* Exactly.
>
> *Liz:*   . . . So it would seem to be a very conflictual situation there.
>
> *Shona:* And that had to be resolved and the management had to be
> almost totally changed. So that was the key job for me – to get
> that environment shifted so that the leadership was in tune with
> that vision.

All Shona's approaches to decision-making were underpinned by 'getting the issue clear or [clarifying] what kind of decision' was needed, before she considered which 'kinds of options [may exist] for addressing' the prob-lem. Developing a thinking 'frame' from a 'substantial analysis' helped her decision-making, as did judicious use of advocacy strategies.

Canada produced two institutional examples of challenges associated with great change. Dominique Abrioux led Athabasca University (a single-mode institution) through a decade of significant growth and change. The challenges came externally and internally. In the early period of his first term as President/Vice-chancellor, provincial government officials showed a lack of understanding about Athabasca's functions and potential, expressing serious concern with 'what they saw [as] very low output from Athabasca, very low enrolments, no graduate studies, and high cost per full-time equivalent'. The future of the university could not be taken for granted.

Internally then, Dominique's overall challenge was to 'provide leadership to a single-mode distance institution whose future was in doubt'. Specifically, that meant becoming more cost-effective, using better economies of scale ('more students . . . into the same courses and the same programmes'). It also meant greater control over fee-setting and 'gaining internal support and approval very early on for a clear-focused strategic university plan'. Added tasks were managing low morale and less than effective labour relations, encouraging all staff to focus on the future of the institution, reorganizing faculty members into flexible, cooperative groups amenable to innovative action, adopting e-learning as a 'complementary' format to print and other media, and streamlining communications between upper management and the faculty and staff. Research into distance education, not just its good practice, had to be strengthened.

Externally, it was imperative to improve relations with the government and clarify the university's mandate *vis-à-vis* the differing academic clienteles and the government's evaluation criteria. Over a three-year period a 31 per cent budget cut had affected the university's search for markets and its structuring of fees. At the municipal government level, the town officials were unhappy and disappointed that the administration's move to their area had not produced a campus with 'live' student activity. Dominique focused his efforts on:

> [identifying] what is our core strength, what . . . nobody else can do. That was all around what I call individualized distance education, which means open: you can start at the first day of any month, you can go at your own speed; all kinds of provisions for students to complete their course and their degree.

For his second five years, a major challenge focused on 'managing quality education and continued growth, not just without government funding but without unused capacity'. The growth rate had to be 10 per cent. The unused capacity had to come from shifting more institutional and course interactions to students working online, for example, using diagnostic tools and library searching; thus reducing staff numbers: 'We changed the way in which students could help themselves.' His work on the next strategic plan would use more slower-paced and collaborative input and greater attention to learners from the very earliest stages of drafting. He had to supervise (successfully) the university through a complex evaluation process for accreditation in the USA and conduct negotiations with other provincial education officials regarding transfer of credit, prior learning assessments, etc. A more pervasive challenge became evident as he prepared to leave the presidency – to recognize the signals of an initially innovative university becoming more traditional, wanting to 'slow down and tread water'.

Ian Mugridge worked through many challenges associated with developing the Open Learning Institute in British Columbia (BC). They arose in response to the education minister's personal passion for rapidly expanding distance-learning opportunities across BC. 'Setting up an institution that nobody [in conventional universities] wanted' was, for Ian, the broad postsecondary context in which he had to set up the degree programme. He did meet this 'considerable challenge' while 'talking [his] way into the system' and managing conditions of 'at best, suspicion, and, at worst, downright hostility'. A major decision was later made to merge several distance-mode independent organizations in BC to create the Open Learning Agency (OLA). That decision created additional new challenges, for example, the growth of a 'divided house', with arguments between staff groups managing different service functions and competing for resources. Glen Farrell had to pursue various challenges as he later led the OLA: to change how teaching and learning occurred in the provincial higher education system; to be a more learner-responsive institution; and to both give and be seen to give added value to the BC postsecondary system. Despite major institutional efforts to sustain quality control of courses, providing a 'basket' of learning services, successful public graduation ceremonies, and partnering and brokering courses, there were various external political, economic and educational factors working against his staff's best efforts. Also evident in society at large was a 'Chamber of Commerce mentality' – business and commercial interests wanted to see impressive bricks and mortar places of higher learning in their communities. Glen's appraisal of some internal challenges was this:

> with hindsight, I just should have done what the first principal . . . did. 'Okay, here [are] some things that we'd like to do, we're not going to do.' But, you know, it's like being a Saskatchewan farmer: you hope next year will be better. So you're reluctant to cut everything off or you're reluctant to lob off any parts of your vision if you think there's a chance that, downstream, you might be able to pursue it.

'When people hire you for your vision, ask to see the books!' Janet Poley's biggest challenge after being hired as the new President and CEO of the American Distance Education Consortium (ADEC) was to clear a surprise US $250 million deficit from faulty auditing. The 'roughest year of [her] life' was spent fixing it, with help from ADEC member universities. Making up this deficit, managing the obligations of federally funded distance education projects, and setting new accounting standards all needed excruciating levels of attention, '. . . so the challenge was how do you come out of that kind of a deficit situation, pick up a moving train, *and* [her emphasis] try to help move things forward in a new and visionary kind of way'. The 'train' of tasks also included teaching member institutions how to conduct quality distance education programming and service delivery, figuring out how to best use the emerging internet, and adapting to a massive increase in satellite fees for course delivery. Some job-sharing to ease the financial management burden, substituting some people for money via their gifts of skill and time, and establishing a creative, skilled 'programme panel' helped to '[multiply] the ability to help us see through these problems'.

Across the Atlantic, Ros Morpeth, as Executive Director of the National Extension College (NEC), had to meet some similar challenges of building up its financial stability (especially given its reliance on self-generated funding), strengthening enrolments while 'growing organically', and responding very quickly to the changing needs of adult learners. A major first task was to restore the NEC's founding focus on distance-mode programmes, followed by substantially increasing the enrolments 'to a level that made it viable to keep on investing and bringing in good people'. Her first decade at NEC, when in charge of course production, presented three challenges: matching course materials design to effective learning; giving educationally appropriate feedback to course authors; and meeting stress-inducing production deadlines. Her final challenge at NEC was the collaborative planning with staff for integrating NEC's operations under a new and bigger (literal) roof.

In reviewing his work in two leadership settings, Raj Dhanarajan used 'people, finance, products and politics' to categorize his challenges. For seven years he helped the Open Learning Institute of Hong Kong (OLIHK), now the Open University of Hong Kong, work through its own internal changes toward providing education appropriate to the cultural and economic needs of Hong Kong citizens and also manage the impacts of the impending Chinese assumption of power. Raj faced three pressing contextual challenges: an influx of foreign advisers trying to impose their own cultural opinions on OLIHK's educational planning; local people accustomed to a colonial culture but needing to develop their own sense of responsibility for their society's development; and the democratizing, liberating ideals of the education OLIHK wanted to promote, to 'enable them to benefit from the economic changes and climate, and a whole range of things, in order to be participants in democracy, to have their voices heard'. So in addition to judiciously moving those OLIHK ideals into acceptance by higher levels of the colony's administration, Raj framed his own challenge:

> What is good practice to help a highly motivated population which was attempting to acquire credentials and qualifications as quickly as possible?; so if they had to [quickly leave Hong Kong] they were going to carry with them a bunch of qualifications that were portable . . .

Later, at the Commonwealth of Learning (COL), Raj faced the same categories of challenge but in different forms. COL needed more staff. It needed to better align its services and products to its mission of helping (British) Commonwealth countries further develop distance education. It had suffered a reduction in political confidence, and then funding, from its major sponsors. Over several years, his challenges increased to include keeping the institutional memory (held in the existing staff) until a collaborative assessment of skill needs was made *vis-à-vis* the requirements of client countries. The results gave staff the opportunity to render services appropriate to the new demands and until those demands had been met. In Raj's terms, such rendering was multi-layered:

> . . . the Commonwealth was demanding, 'How do we improve the quality of our distance education and open learning, from quality in terms of products, quality in terms of student support systems, quality in terms of management?' . . . How do you shape your organization to help . . . the Open University in Tanzania put in place its quality assurance framework; not by just sending a consultant to write a report but doing more than that actually: ensuring that those people would have a responsibility to manage quality, had the necessary training, had the necessary literature, had an opportunity to see other systems in practice?

One example of a complex mix of administrative and leadership challenges emerged in Claire Matthewson's reflections. After building up a strong community network for sustaining new, audio-conferenced programmes and gaining the necessary acceptance by University of Otago staff and faculty members, she led the development of distance mode higher education across the South Pacific. Her key task over five years at the University of the South Pacific was to support the distance education directors in each of the 12 countries. Linguistic, logistical, political and educational issues formed a turbulent mix of challenges: 265 distinct languages in 60 different cultures with English as the only common (if only as third or fourth) language; sending study materials for 17,000 learners out and back over 33 million sq km of small islands with poor communication networks; mediating intellectual property and other conflicts between academics and course designers; negotiating policy development with 12 Ministers of Education; stopping the administrators' practice of using distance education courses as the 'rehabilitation' process for academically troubled students; and addressing women's reduced entry into higher education. The list could be longer, but its impacts were offset by human determination: 'The learning demand was so huge and, against great odds, everyone wanted to make it work.'

Ulrich Bernath's encapsulation of his challenges in setting up a new Centre for Distance Education at Carl von Ossietzky University of Oldenburg, in 1978, are not dissimilar to the experience of many of his colleagues in this study. In setting up the Centre, he aimed to build capacity toward setting up distance education service and support units in conventional universities. To some extent, he had to 'swim' against the traditional university 'streams' of teaching practice and societal respectability. He had to focus on making educational change and constantly and creatively negotiating for more funds to survive and expand. 'Collaborating with motivated people to do exactly what the establishment is not expecting them to do' takes ingenuity and an unshakeable passion for the cause.

Course design and production

A contextual note is needed here. This topic has been discussed much over the past 40 years in distance education. Course design, as an institutional concept and a multi-skill team-based process, operated widely in pre-internet decades. Single-mode institutions (i.e. exclusively distance mode, as in various 'open universities') relied on sending their students detailed, comprehensive, highly structured, cognitively interactive, peer-evaluated, mixed-media learning materials. Considerable staff resources were consumed in this design and production, but the process often enhanced the teaching skills of academics and showcased exemplary resource-based teaching to external critics as well as to consumers in other post-secondary institutions. The rationale for such work and its costs was based on the argument that the pre-designed presentation of course content and its associated learning activities had to carry most of the teaching function. Personal tutorial support by academically skilled and trained tutors was provided, but learner and tutor essentially worked from the same materials. Course materials had to be designed, revised and produced to strict schedules, in the days before software and other technologies emerged to save time and effort. In other contexts, for example, using audio- or video-conferencing, or online activity, more flexibility existed for guiding learners and adding content.

Generally, when detailed course materials were sent to students, the assumed need to lecture was removed (indeed was actively discouraged by distance education advisers). The roles of tutors were to help their group of learners work through structured activities, discuss the course content, and helpfully grade written assignments within specified time limits.

How, therefore, did the interviewees reflect on their chief challenges regarding course designs? Two major foci emerged: teaching skill development and the promotion of effective learning.

Teaching skill development

Daryl Nation had to admit that he entered distance mode teaching in the 1970s with some scepticism: 'It had to be a patched up set of circumstances.' Soon he became 'committed' to interactive teaching with students who valued the opportunity to take a course off campus. He quickly learned that faculty development, especially for distance mode teaching skills, was an imperative, albeit 'a difficult and challenging exercise'. Brian Kenworthy would agree on that last point. His consulting in universities and vocational colleges often placed him at the uncomfortable intersection of others' unreflective habit and unsought change. He had to help 'lecturers' entering distance mode contexts change their 'mindset' from assuming that distance education meant merely replicating face-to-face classroom lecturing in a new form (old wine in new bottles). The challenge was how to encourage traditional academics to become more deliberative and informed about the design of interactive learning. Difficult also were his challenges in delivering course materials to remote learners whose contexts posed significant communications challenges. Chère Gibson echoed other comments about the need to gain support from faculty members and the administration when looking for faculty willing to learn how to teach by distance.

Staff development as a key driver and supporter of change was one of many challenges given to Louise Moran when in the role of managing a new university operation. She was responsible for producing extensive innovations in cost-effective, multi-mode teaching modes. The broad goal was to help the university 'do a great deal more with a great deal less' as it struggled to react to reduced government funding and government demands to increase enrolments:

> The [centre] was charged to help the faculties move into a new realm of teaching and learning, with an emphasis on curriculum and [quality assurance] driven by graduate outcomes. The [centre] had to be a change agent for the whole university and the ambition was that the university would change dramatically its capacity to meet the needs of students in a very fast-changing environment for professional education.

Very different sets of staff skills had to be amalgamated. Staff skilled in distance mode course design and the management of student records, advising of on-campus students, faculty teaching skill development and campuswide applications of multimedia (audio-visual) had to learn to come together, as quickly as possible. Revenue generation was expected, as was developing research capacity. The 'classic divide and snobbery' between academics and professional and technical staff was evident. Professional staff had become so overloaded with correcting and updating existing distance mode courses that they could not help new faculty develop courses or plan a curriculum. Finally, the centre had to involve itself in the university's international development initiatives.

Moving now to interpersonal challenges faced in course design, consider these examples. In taking faculty members and courses into the new online environment, Gary Miller ensured that each faculty member for each course worked with an instructional designer to ease the path. Access to special funding enabled faculty innovators to claim ownership of their innovations and teach their colleagues how to teach online. Gail Crawford's early experience as an instructional designer helped her learn to manage the analysis of the design problems with the content expert (otherwise known as the professor or instructor):

> My first problem is to figure out, with you, your discipline, your students and what our resources are to get there, what we are trying to accomplish, and what tools have we got. And then we can start pulling together a plan for what this course should consist of. What elements do we have to build or buy or seek out? What resources can we put into play? And then we develop our plan for action. And then you and I would each

have some responsibilities. You would produce an assembly of the curriculum, the material, the information you want to teach and we would work together building the guiding objectives or goals.

Also influencing Gail's interaction style was her assessment of how the instructor might react to her suggestions:

My problem with you would be probably the same now as it was 30 years ago and that is [that] you may be more or less open to hearing ideas about how to accomplish these jobs. If you are a straight 'sage on the stage' style faculty person or an instructivist then you are going to hear some ideas, and if you are a diehard constructivist person then you are going to hear some other ones. The reality . . . is that as a consultant, you have to work with people where they are.

The location of faculty members' experience and career advancement needs could vary greatly. The inexperienced ones often posed the challenge of being inarticulate about required learning outcomes. Those wanting to maintain their reputation could easily write too much content, resulting in producing 'nice to know' supplementary material (as distinct from student-preferred 'need to know' material). (This point was echoed strongly by Fred Lockwood.) As an instructional design consultant, Gail had multiple challenges, not least to find a delicate balance between pragmatic, limited content provision and more idealistic approaches to help students who were committed to the discipline to engage deeply.

Promoting effective learning

Karlene Faith was very clear about her challenge at the dual mode Simon Fraser University while teaching as an academic at the same time as advising her peers on distance mode learning design. It was to remain 'absolutely focused on the students' need for what they experience as personal attention in a routine, structured, predictable, timely fashion'. Similarly, working for the now-named Distance Education and Training Council (DETC) in the USA, Michael Lambert's challenge remains that of helping member institutions keep a strong focus on learners and learning, if for no other reason than the fact that satisfied students help institutional finances. But maintaining high academic standards carried its own difficulties as he worked with members eager to maintain their DETC accreditation: 'Sometimes, it's not the most profitable thing in the world to require up-to-date material and sufficient number of faculty and to give top service – those are expensive things, but I learned to be righteous about it.' Relevance of course content to learners' interests could become a challenge when international providers were involved. Failing to adequately revise materials designed in another culture is one issue (Ronnie Carr). Facing cultural differences in course formats or philosophical differences in 'the contingency of knowledge', as

Dan Granger at Empire State College had to learn, calls for negotiation or walking away.

Effective learning also may be impaired when gender-related issues are not taken into account, as Gisela Pravda learnt in conducting 'obligatory' evaluations of distance mode courses for the BIBB – Bundesinstitut für Berufsbildung (Federal Institute for Vocational Education) in Germany and in planning education activities in Colombia. The choice of language and illustrative examples of concepts or skill performance may influence how 'welcome' and competent women students feel in a course. The challenge therefore is to educate people to accept the need for non-sexist, gender-inclusive language, gender-appropriate course content and 'gender-sensitive didactics', without regression to a superficial 'add women and stir' approach.

Working in or for developing countries challenged several interviewees. David Warr, for example, faced one senior university administrator whose inability to grasp the societal value of David's projects (developing functional literacy around the country) created deliberate administrative hindrances. Finding a course design and an appropriate mix of visual and audio materials to relate to hundreds of simultaneous study groups for huge numbers of mostly illiterate students was another challenge. Whenever printed study materials had to be produced, David's ongoing challenge, across all his international contexts, was to help course writers, some of them academics, 'come down to the right level; stop assuming people know things, and explain'.

Perceived equivalence of quality in teaching and learning with conventional higher education standards was a serious challenge for many respondents. Consider international development, for example:

> an awful lot of my time in Lagos and in Namibia was spent arguing . . . with traditional academics that [what] one was doing in terms of opening up opportunities by distance education was A, respectable, and B, feasible. That battle is still [having] to be fought in many countries in Africa: 'What is this open learning stuff? It is not proper education.'
>
> (Tony Dodds)

Even when high-quality distance mode operations are successfully established, covert doubts about the mode itself may linger, as Greville Rumble noted while discussing developing countries:

> even if the policy-makers and government tick the right boxes and articulate the right policies (e.g. distance education qualifications have equal validity with traditional qualifications; students can transfer between distance and traditional programmes, carrying credit with them), it does not mean that distance education *per se* will be accepted by academics, or by students, or by employers. So every society has, in the end, to fight its own battles for validity and acceptance.

National-level education development was not immune. Gisela Pravda and Bernd Schachstiek had to work hard to prove how new course standards and accreditation procedures could transform an earlier reputation. As Gisela remarked, 'We were giving distance education a professional standard' and especially 'from a consumers' protection standpoint'.

Challenges of equivalence were mentioned variously. Donald McDonell insisted that the quality of distance mode teaching and learning in his university be of exactly the same standard, if not better than, traditional on-campus teaching. Ronnie Carr, in managing open entry and public credibility issues as Dean of the School of Education and Languages at OUHK never 'succumbed' to reducing his 'high exit standards' for graduating students. Ian Mugridge's use of a scaled down version of the Open University (UK) course development team process demanded a content expert, external validators and an instructional designer: 'You know, the usual sort of course writing process.' That 'process' and its products built respect from conventional universities, facilitating discipline-based articulation which eased his courses into the existing higher education system and improved credit transfer into the same system.

Learner needs

Here, access, equity of treatment, and tutoring and guidance were particular sites of challenge.

Naomi (Sargant) McIntosh's challenge in establishing educational programming for Channel 4 in the UK was to create psychologically safe ways of thinking about living and learning. Since her intended viewing audience, not carrying higher education credentials, would not respond well to academically styled programmes, she challenged herself to design attractive 'labels' for her programme strands:

> The strand for the unemployed I labelled 'For people with more time than money'. [The] strand . . . about basic skills . . . was called 'Living in a brown envelope world' – all your communications are coming to you in official envelopes, and you have no basic skills to deal with official envelopes.

However, her solution to counter some notions of postsecondary education as forbidding ('doomy') posed a subsequent challenge. An academic in critical evaluation mode argued with her that such programming was not properly educational and should carry formal academic titles. Naomi's justification was crisp and clear: 'because we had to reach out'.

From the late 1970s Gary Miller was using broadcasting to overcome '[an] incredible mish mash of [media-based] delivery restrictions' concerning courses needed by adults living in the less-privileged 'hills and hollows of Appalachia'. So cable television and satellite technology applications were designed to enhance flexibility of delivery to different audiences: 'On one hand, we could use satellite to deliver very specific education to very specific audiences and on the other hand we could use cable television to reach out to broader audiences over a broader geographic area.' As Naomi planned value-added learning 'extras' for UK Channel 4 broadcasts, Gary developed extra experiences to meet his challenge of 'creating an educated viewer'. Taken as a whole, as evidence of learner-centred innovation, directing the following kinds of activities created 'an exciting time' for Gary: viewing groups and study booklets; managing Penn State University professors travelling to rural libraries for community programming; and giving opportunities for learners to ease into credit courses.

Donald McDonell was morally exercised if he did not resolve his key challenge of increasing access and interaction for students regardless of their location, and without descent into transmission modes of teaching (lectures):

> There are students in the off-campus centres who want to follow a course but can't make it to campus. There are all these courses being taught every night on campus. There must be a way to make use of the new technologies appearing on the market to connect the two groups together in a way that would create a quality learning environment in the off-campus centres without having a negative effect in the on-campus classroom.

Judith Fage, as Regional Director, London Region of the OUUK, led the care and management of 20,000 adult students and all associated staff and tutor support procedures. She retained her attention to learner needs as various administrative and leadership challenges claimed her energies. Some challenges related to integration of staff and resources, internal competency models, the huge scale of OUUK systems, and inter-agency politicking inside the OUUK. Her list of the associated challenges follows.

- Living with the imposition of 'covert management agendas'.
- Confronting the intensive work needed to upgrade student records software and systems ('intellectually quite difficult and at times extremely tedious').
- Upgrading Equal Opportunity codes for practice (especially against harassment).
- Managing the staff reduction impacts of annually shrinking budgets.
- Handling a 'highly controversial' contract for one category of staff critical to student success.
- Implementing European human rights legislation.
- Setting standards for the general (non-tutoring) guidance of students, especially to meet the needs of new groupings of students taking professional development courses.
- Leading the design of new offices.

Earlier, as a Senior Counsellor [sic] in the OUUK, Judith had faced institutional issues associated with the guidance of students. These included managing the commitment and skill development of part-time tutorial staff, developing and implementing 'student support and guidance policy and practice', adhering to new procedures for supporting equal opportunity practices (spearheaded in the OUUK by Lee Taylor in the early 1990s), researching new career guidance activities for some regional students, and, later, in the early 1990s, developing web-based guidance for students. Change in the external higher education context was a partial stimulant, as well as major expansion inside the OUUK itself:

> in the higher education sector in the UK . . . we were moving into the 30 per cent–40 per cent [participation rate] by that time – it was a huge expansion. And partly in response to that, but partly in response to a kind of mood or process of professionalization everywhere in university student support and guidance, we had to transform [almost] a cottage industry into a well-developed and comprehensive system.

Student counselling, as a 'continuity of concern' platform in the general infrastructures of the OUUK, had to be refined in its earliest applications. Not an easy task to analyse, though, as Greville Rumble explained: 'What is the boundary between advising someone on difficulties in finding time to study, and advising someone because their partner/spouse is angry at the time they are taking studying? It's not always clear, especially to someone wrapped up in a student's problem.' In the large regions, in the small communities, Roger Mills's early experience helped him learn that adults wanting a second chance at higher education needed 'a better deal' and more than just design excellence in course materials. So he led the establishment of a regional guidance service that became a forerunner for current OUUK services. To provide some service flexibility, since not all students took a complete programme, he also led the introduction of an associate student counsellor for those students: 'We were constantly pushing the administration for different ways of doing things.'

Enabling distance students' engagement with learning, without face-to-face contact, commanded the attention of various participants. Judith George's narrative, for example, shows how she met learners on their own psychological ground:

> The first assignment had come due, and this particular person whom I hadn't met hadn't turned in an assignment. I got a letter saying, 'I'm terribly sorry, but it's a very early lambing this year.' I thought, 'great, this is fantastic . . . this student striding all over the hills at all hours of the day' . . . the . . . study is firing people up so they could do their familiar, more mundane work, but also could engage and stretch their minds as well.

Such attention to learners also means being alert to psychological 'turbulence' associated with significant learning. The classic distance education movie, *Educating Rita*, showed how engagement in higher education may influence, profoundly, an adult's behaviour, relationships and interests. Judith responded to such adults who struggled to link old contexts and new thinking:

... a woman who was a blue collar worker on a shop floor ... was quite distressed, three months into the course, because she was beginning to find her vocabulary was changing. And she said 'I've got to deliberately stop myself using certain terms, because it would seem to my friends and neighbours very posh.' And she was beginning to find herself in situations that needed variety in the type of discourse used – the way in which you have different registers for different contexts. This was the first time she had come across this demand, and found it not only difficult, but also somehow false. I felt that you've got to really listen hard to people and be very supportive because what you were helping them to do was very exciting, but was also potentially very destructive. It was very turbulent. All serious education changes the learner; and education for many adults, shoehorned into a tightly restricted life, could be deeply disturbing for them and for their friends and family.

To end, the reputational issue

This issue links to the quality equivalence issue. Many participants confronted negative public attitudes toward 'correspondence' and 'distance' education. Three main sources of negativity were identified. The general public and many traditional university academics and administrators were highly sceptical that any higher education that was not based on face-to-face and time-bound lectures in a walled classroom could not qualify as being high in quality or popularity: 'Correspondence education' in various countries had become 'disreputable' when run by 'commercial correspondence cultures who varied from the pretty shoddy to the dishonest' (Hilary Perraton). The canon of open admission ('apply any time, any place, and we will help you succeed') and the discarding of elitist notions that students had to meet entrance requirements 'into' the halls of academe meant for some doubters that failures of distance-mode students and institutional credibility would be inevitable.

The battles for reputation fought by participants involved gaining the resources and skills to produce learning and teaching materials of very high quality, providing trained tutorial and guidance services, revealing advantageous statistics for course grades and drop-out rates and telling student success stories, all while managing public scepticism or even hostility without becoming defensive. For today's higher education contexts, participants believe that the reputation of distance education, as they traditionally understand the term, has been much improved. The often assumed use of the term 'online education' as a linguistic replacement for all that the term 'distance education' entails for the participants may be an influencing factor, but it needs further and critical study. The positive change in public status and increased safety from the actions of detractors and disbelievers, however, does not necessarily guarantee safety from predators.

And therein lies an irony with which to end this chapter. After all the challenges of distance education's overall quality, academic credibility, institutional or departmental management, revenue generation, and teaching effectiveness have been met, after experiential wisdom and experience have accumulated, a further challenge may lurk for the unwary. Colin Yerbury had to manage it in his university: 'academic units that saw a success story and then wanted [the distance education operation] for themselves'.

3

Guiding their practice: access, respect and responsiveness

Liz Burge

Overall, participant responses focused on equitable access to education, respect for and responsiveness to learners and their contexts, deliberatively engaging learning materials, and collegial management. Various personal principles and action preferences supported these professional ideals.

Equitable access

Creating and enhancing access to postsecondary education elicited the most responses. Words such as 'fundamental', 'core', 'very strong', 'passion', and 'absolute' characterized the intensity of valuing access. You will note some sources for such beliefs in the self-written biographies.

Access depends in part on openness by institutions and/or the levels of resources under the command of potential students. Several participants revealed their own elitist education and its benefits, while others had experienced their own 'closed doors' and therefore wanted to build open doors to learning, not to mention the support needed to walk through them to academic success:

> So it becomes a sort of equalitarian thing . . . It is because I grew up in an extremely poor Liverpool background . . . Was enormously lucky to go to grammar school and university, and then the US as a graduate student, all on scholarships. And have ended up the middle-class professional person I am because I was given access to [education].
>
> (John Thomas)

> The number of opportunities that people like me got to have a university education was a disgrace. When I went to university, 2 per cent of every age group, on average, went to university. And if you were part of the 2 per cent, that was wonderful; but what if you weren't? That was your loss. And so I think that [what] the Open University started is . . . a wonderful thing, and I genuinely, firmly believe in what the OU and the

other open universities and [the British Columbia Open University] did.

(Ian Mugridge)

. . . having a sense of social justice is important to me. I don't want to see other people deprived.

(David Hawkridge)

Janet Poley, for example, 'loves creative projects that . . . have the opportunity to make a big difference in people's lives' (and especially minority populations). To her, access to education is a major determinant in making such a difference. Naomi Sargant and her pioneering colleagues at the Open University (OUUK) used the example of 'the crofter [small farmer] on the Isle of Mull' as a guide to designing accessible learning materials for geographically isolated learners.

Several participants echoed Ronnie Carr's concern about the managerialism in higher education. Consider how he phrased his thinking:

I find some of the management talk that goes on in education quite difficult to accept. All this talk about consumers and cost efficiency and gaining a competitive edge; I don't feel comfortable with it. I don't deny that such changes are taking place but I don't see why I need to just fall into line with [them]. I believe very firmly in opening up education. I've seen many examples of people who on the surface don't look as if they are likely to perform well or benefit from higher education. But after they have learned the tricks of the trade . . . they can do extremely well.

Others believed, as part of the access process, that learners have a right to step away, easily and fault-free, from learning opportunities if or when they believe that such action best suits their needs. Judith Fage's unchanged and 'very profound' belief that 'there ought to be something there for everyone' referred to the positive 'potential' inherent in adult learners and their corresponding right to 'have a go at something that they aspire to even if [later they decide that] it isn't right for them'. Bernd Schachtsiek and his staff thought in a similar way: they 'loved' their 'happy drop-outs' who felt free to cancel their course without any implications of personal failure and accompanied only by invitations to return to study when convenient.

Access is linked conceptually with beating boundaries and ensuring that flexibility is built into the use of various types of 'places' – psychological, socioeconomic and geographical. Chère Gibson argued that her university's mantra, 'The boundaries of the university are the boundaries of the state', influenced the reach of her programming. In her mind, paying state taxes automatically gives every adult the right to flexible access to education that is relevant to those adults' goals. Shona Butterfield phrased the flexibilities inherent in distance education as 'at your own pace and in your own place'.

John Thomas was not the only person to point to the differential access issue when voicing his concerns about the use of electronic media in developing countries. Greville Rumble is concerned about equitable access by those who face very diminished living conditions and expectations, regardless of country:

> How are we going to manage getting a fairer society in places like Africa and parts of Asia – and indeed in the US and the UK? You know, we'll go on and on trying to have growth economies, and we'll face increasingly severe environmental problems. So I'm driven now by wondering how the hell one builds something that's going to be sustainable and of reasonable quality and that's going to meet the needs of the poor, and help them have better lives, and help develop a sustainable pattern of life . . .

Lord Geoffrey Crowther's explanations of the four guiding aspects of openness – to people, places, methods, and ideas – used in his founding Chancellor's speech for the official opening of the OUUK on 23 July 1969, were recalled by Naomi (Sargant) McIntosh as 'an absolutely evocative set of words' and ideas that infused her idealism and that of her colleagues. Roger Mills used the same words as 'not just a slogan'. In his early regional work for the OUUK, he modelled them in two key principles of maintaining 'collegiate' management and recognizing the diversity of the student and the tutor bodies of the OUUK. He quickly realized that 'this [diversity] was an absolutely explosive mixture for innovative and exciting teaching in the study centres'. His use of collaboration and team working within the OUUK extended into his relationships with other regional providers, all of whom were competing actively and openly against each other. Roger's belief that 'you have to collaborate to compete' grew from his daily experience with various providers all looking to build access opportunities for adults. Long a fan of the OUUK's work to promote high quality tutoring, Ulrich Bernath analysed then current politically left ideas for opening up access opportunities to education and realized that 'this new distance teaching university, the FernUniversität, was a step in this right direction and that distance education, which I didn't know anything about before, is the key'.

Judith George's critical thinking about the conventional praising of students, based on their successful struggle to 'jump through . . . various hoops', i.e. institutional regulations and expectations, led her to devise her own guiding questions that reversed the focus: 'these are people who want to learn – what do they want to learn, how can we provide what they want?'

From access as inclusion in macro-level education systems we move to the micro-level of the learner's inclusion in learning materials and teaching processes.

Respect for and responsiveness to learners' needs

Respect for what each learner brings to learning – for example, their context, goals, expectations, fears, growth potential, or inhibiting 'baggage' – acts as a consistent theme. Every participant, at some time during their interview, articulated their commitment to role-modelling respect, even when the 'r' word was not directly used. Two short narratives capture the scope of learners' contexts that command such respect. The first follows here and the second is at the chapter's end.

> We [had] been holding a series of evening lectures to celebrate the fifteenth anniversary of the university. Our school organized a talk by a prominent professor of Chinese literature from another university in Hong Kong. When I watched people going into the lecture theatre, I saw a familiar face, the cleaner [of my office carpet]. She even stayed at the end of the lecture to ask the speaker some questions. The next day she told me that she had also been to the previous lecture in the series on 'Mathematics in everyday life'. And then [she] said 'Thank you for helping me to learn.' I don't mind telling you that this brought a tear to my eyes. Providing opportunities for people like this is what open education should be about.
>
> (Ronnie Carr)

As Dan Granger explained his guiding belief, being responsive to learners' needs and contexts is 'quite different from the notion that knowledge is fixed and can be made available in a generic format for a multitude of learners'. To him, it involves an educational form of social activism in its use of accessible, appropriate learning designs and learning spaces, all capitalizing on the 'abundance of information and the dynamic nature of knowledge'. Gail Crawford uses a different angle on the same theme of respect: she wants to maintain the canons of traditional distance education practice:

> I just don't want the fundamental qualities of distance education, as we've developed it, to be lost; [i.e.] the real, important, and sometimes unique attitudes that include 'beginning with the learner', making provision for variations and flexibility, reducing bureaucratic processes, and conducting the teaching and learning activities in ways that give students the best possible chance to succeed.

Part of Hilary Perraton's interest in better-quality distance education sprang from his concern about when responsiveness fails; this time expressed as a learner writing letters asking for someone to explain why she or he had failed an examination quite some time previously. Failure of respect due to learners in Fred Lockwood's view may mean failing ourselves as well as the learner if practitioners 'don't give them the best' or waste their time. So he focuses on 'the really important person, and to me it's that person who is coming from work, has spent well-earned money to start this course, [is managing] all the other pressures, [has] family around him [or her]; cutting out time to study this course. It's not easy.' During his early days in US distance education, Michael Lambert gained much guidance from 'fearless' colleagues who carried 'this sense of high purpose about defending the consumer's right to a good education at a fair price, and the right to be well treated'.

Overall, service to learners was a very strong guiding theme. Even when the scale of the operation was large, service was construed as what actually happened to individuals (as distinct from intentions). As Bernd Schachtsiek argued about his organization, 'we have more than a thousand teachers, but we treat each of our 60,000 students [as if he or she] is the only one'.

Deliberatively engaging learning materials

Much of the experience represented here from the interviews does not refer to today's ubiquitous use of online learning. Three reasons may apply: online technology was not seen as a key factor for answering the question about guides to practice; widespread use of the internet had not been a feature over the participant's career; and some participants had worked in countries where procuring even enough paper and pencils for text-literate learners was a real challenge.

Second-chance learning for adults cannot mean second-rate learning or teaching. While Ian Mugridge, working in a single-mode distance institution, believed in 'providing an alternative way of approaching higher education [he did not], however, believe in a second-rate alternative'. Design for quality guided the experience of participants who commented here. Sustained deliberation about how students would most effectively learn within their own life loads and contexts informed the design of learning and its academic support. John Cowan's principle, for example, of building reciprocal trust between him and his students links to his second key principle of thinking from the student's point of view – to the point of 'pushing myself into the learner role'.

Parity of learning and teaching conditions and expectations was expressed by several as a guiding principle. Distance mode teaching in dual-mode institutions (i.e., synchronous, face-to-face, 'traditional' teaching as well as distance mode delivery) had to be seen and proven to be equal in demands and quality: 'No qualitative difference between on-campus and off-campus teaching' should occur, and especially when mediated by audio-conferencing technologies (Donald McDonell).

Many participants referred, in various ways, to a steady focus on integrating all the components of learner, learning materials, technologies, and teaching services. A focus only on the materials, as if they alone would adequately sustain a learner, was mentioned overtly by several as misguided and inadequate practice. Tony Bates's two beliefs here represent others' opinions:

> I really believe in distance education as a very effective means of teaching but it has to be done well . . . You can pour millions into course production but if you don't have good learner support the system falls

down. I do believe in good interaction between teacher and student and between students.

Learners' preferences and technology capacities should influence how course designers choose and integrate course activities, as Claire Matthewson explained in relation to technology selection:

> Looking at different learning styles . . . we have students who have difficulty getting access; we have students who can't afford access to internet-type things; we have students who live in places where it doesn't quite work. We have people who don't learn well that way; they learn better by discussion and talking. None of these things is 'die-in-the-ditch' compulsory but, as you know, in every learning group, you'll get people who actually prefer to or happen to learn better in one way than another. So where possible, we offer a range of technologies. Looking at our particular market segment, however – particularly high-end professionals who learn a lot from listening and talking to one another – at the end of a working day interacting with technology, the last thing they want to do is log on to the internet. Looking at the screen at night, when you've been doing it all day, isn't always helpful. But they will 'attend' a discussion about a critical problem.

Colin Yerbury's view is that 'it has to be a combination of print/online interaction, as well as still having telephone access to an instructor'. A Canadian peer of his believes in a blended approach of 'complementary components' and still uses a heuristic of three questions to guide his thinking about course functionality: 'What are the characteristics of the target learners? What's the nature of the content? and How much money have you got? And out of that one distils the art of the possible in terms of the various methodologies that one can use' (Glen Farrell). In New Zealand, Shona Butterfield's experience in nursing education had led her to different interrogating questions: 'I was always very open to thinking about where were the learners, what was their context, and what could I bring to bear to make that learning experience work? Would it be multimedia?'

Various other criteria for directed, deliberate engagement emerged, and in part they related to the fact that some participants had been assisting adults who either needed a second chance after failing at school age or did not ever assume that they could be successful in higher education. Specifically, three criteria mentioned were these: gaining learner interest, clearly written course content directed to and appropriate for students (not academic peers or rivals) and engaging tone of text: 'I used to edit very ruthlessly . . . and put myself in the position of the student who was reading it' (Janet Jenkins).

John Thomas, whose expertise lay in developing audio- and radio-based learning programmes, quickly learnt that radio was a very powerful but covert stimulant in getting adults even interested in learning:

Mainly you don't try to teach things directly, but rather you get people interested in learning. That learning process can then go on through other media, like follow-up print materials, practical activities and meeting together in groups with other like-minded people.

Using radio for learning, though, takes skill because the scaffolding – the programme design and its script – demand apparently conflicting operational criteria: they need a finely nuanced, clear conceptual structure but that has to be invisible to the listener. Thomas's output criterion for programmes that have to 'represent reality, not reproduce it', was getting a positive affective response from the listener. Each of thousands of listeners would 'feel' natural speech or 'voicing' without any evidence of the extensive 'scaffolding' beneath. Hear the similar guiding criteria of someone whose job, in part, was to assist a group of instructional designers working with faculty members at the OUUK to develop attractive and integrated course guides:

> It's got to speak to somebody; it's got to have a voice to it. It's got to be written in a vein that can be understood by people who are not already into that genre, into that scholarly sphere . . . trying to see it from the student's point of view. [It] has to be looked at from a holistic point of view, every possible angle. And then you comment back to the author, and that becomes an art in itself because authors are sensitive.
>
> (David Hawkridge)

When a distance educator leads an educational company or non-publicly-funded organization (as with members of the European Association of Distance Learning – EADL) and she or he wants to attract and retain large numbers of students, his or her supervision of course design personnel is guided partly by the intended learners' contexts and their reading habits:

> We decided to have two different authors for a course. One was the expert in the field and the other one was somebody who was able to write and to transform the text to the level of the target group. For example, we knew that our target group is not the high skilled university person. Our target group still is the workers in the workplace and they read tabloids for example. So we decided that the language in our courses, especially in the beginning, should be nearer to how journalists write than like an expert would write . . . So [the course] was very easy at the beginning but was on a very high level at the end.
>
> (Bernd Schachtsiek)

Course design is also guided by adults' needs for practical, real-world solutions and interests. Here is an example from the same organization:

> People always need motivation when they learn, so we asked our students: what would you like to learn first? And even if it's not the perfect curriculum, we developed something we called the spiral curriculum. So it's not that they learn the theory and then the practice; we started with

some practice and then explained the theory in the second step . . . Students call them very helpful from the beginning.

(Bernd Schachtsiek)

Other guiding criteria for effective learning discussed were appropriate conceptual scaffolding and meaningfully structured learning activities. When operationalized, they would help learners proactively construct meaning with some degree of skilled independence and confidence in using a repertoire of learning skills. Greville Rumble, speaking this time as a distance mode learner, argued that the key factor for him 'is that one is not being handed something just on a plate. One has to go through a process of mastering it. One has an internal dialogue.' He values learners having 'freedom within structure' for applications of constructivist ways of learning. Teachers who could not put such a philosophy into action, but instead acted like 'parents' or carried a 'Nightingale complex', were not good for business, quite literally, because adult students wanted someone who helped them 'find their own way', as Bernd explained. Terry Gibson, also guided by a focus on building effective and proactive learners, and working with conferencing technologies, argued for helping learners to quickly feel that, in a safe environment, 'they have broken the barrier and managed the technology . . . and that they have begun the engagement process with their fellow learners'.

Meaningful activities take various forms, for example, forms of in-text questioning, multiple choices, summaries of ideas, and culture, age, and gender-sensitive tasks as well as illustrative examples. As a flexible thinker, Gail Crawford encourages her students to independently and critically think about, rather than criticizing, published literature. In her learning 'consultant' role, otherwise known as tutoring, she is guided by a combination of honesty ('absolutely'), 'constructive' feedback and a 'generosity of spirit' that she expects to give to and accept from her students. Her feedback becomes 'generous' when it tactfully gives credit for student work to date and offers feasible, theoretical or strategic alternatives to consider. As with many of her colleagues who respect adult students' time, energies and self-esteem, she stressed the importance of basic courtesies and reasonable and clear expectations – no frivolous or 'silly, repetitive tasks'. Having high standards does not negate caring and respect. As a long-time distance educator, Gail holds firmly to the general guiding principle of creating opportunities for effective learning where it might not have been possible otherwise. Other colleagues also commented on feedback. Typical of the kind of feedback required is this comment from Ronnie Carr: 'Reasonably balanced' feedback in such a style '. . . that it's clear that the writer . . . is not just imposing his or her values on controversial issues'.

Operational guides in designing and sustaining successful courses included piloting of materials, overall 'timeliness and accuracy and consistent quality' (Claire Matthewson), and attention to the small details associated with any course or event. Fred Lockwood stressed the need to 'get all the nitty gritty [logistical details] right' before one small mistake produced cumulating disasters.

As part of his primary guiding principle of 'service' to learners, Bernd Schachtsiek commented on the type of support needed for expeditious handling of student problems. For example, good listeners (in many cases women who have managed the demands of their families) will often act as good problem-solvers for student worries, but the end result must be helpful: '. . . if a student has a problem, take care of it and find a solution'.

Some universities used teams of people, representing skills of conceptualization, content expertise, instructional/learning design, technology application, library skills, editing, copyright clearances, etc. The UK Open University's course teams, supported by significant funding that almost no other institutions could afford, gained much international respect for their detailed work in creating materials of very high quality. Other institutions operating on smaller scales used smaller working groups to produce course materials. Regardless of scale and funding level, the teams' success depended on respectful and effective relationships between team members. In leaving this section, the last word goes to Gary Miller's expression of his key guiding principle:

> Always honouring the student's perspective: that's an important characteristic of anything we might do because the technology will change, the faculty we work with will change, the institutional setting will change; but still we are always trying to achieve change in a student. And understanding the student . . . and being willing to listen to the student, and think about the student first, is a prerequisite to doing this stuff right.

Collegial relationships

Here the reflections referred mostly to institution-based relationships between distance education staff and to relationships with external peers or with non-distance mode peers in the same institution.

Relationships managed by distance education staff, when directly mentioned, reflected the leaders' concerns for mutual respect and understanding. Shona Butterfield felt impelled to 'walk the talk', in addition to knowing and respecting all that constitutes the 'person' and her or his rights to learn and to make mistakes. Dominique Abrioux also was guided by his need to role-model the goals of his institution – to build 'openness and communications and relationships with staff . . . it is not just service to students, it's service to staff'. Tom Prebble believed in taking consistently principled positions for decision-making. They are key for being ethical and for being transparent as a manager: 'certainly when dealing with staff, it's the right way to go; you don't have any secret files on people, you don't run conspiracies against them, you confront issues frankly, directly, rather than covertly'. He would never get himself into a possible and precarious position of being 'found out'. Transparency also was an important 'yardstick' or guiding principle for Raj Dhanarajan's leadership, as were 'honesty' and 'sensitivity' to others and their contexts. Important for Louise Moran were (1) her recognition that staff members are 'whole people' with life roles and demands beyond those dictated by their work; (2) her expectations for responsible behaviour by all staff; and (3) her use, indeed celebration, of diverse professional skills held among staff without her needing personally to match them:

> The trick with managing [staff] is . . . not to have all of their expertise, because you can't and you don't, and you don't want to share this bit of culture and not that, but to challenge them in their own terms and negotiate across those cultures within your group. And . . . give them enough rope to see how far they can take something.

Similarly, Ros Morpeth, in recalling a key mentor's concerns that the organization might become '. . . bureaucratic and unadventurous', used to encourage her staff to be creative and 'to be able to take things forward themselves, rather than be a little cog in a wheel'. Bernd Schachtsiek also appreciated his staff: 'I [love] the people [I] work with because they really make an effort, they have a dream to go for.' Deliberately calm consultative behaviour with her staff helped Judith Fage introduce change or innovation, even though at times it meant her giving repeated explanations about a proposed change and a declaration of respectful disagreement with any laggards once the changes began.

Professional peer relationships were valued widely. In his international development work, David Warr developed reports on project activities that enabled local colleagues to reflect on their work and contribute to its documentation. He sought their input and helped build their report-writing skills as he helped them to see 'the good things and the problems'. Such collaborative strategies were evidence of his underlying, guiding principle of '[achieving] something, something that is sustainable after I have gone. If we work together in the same direction and I'll try to steer that direction and throw in some information.'

Sometimes, relationships with peers external to one's institution were experienced as a psychological security blanket. Conferences, for example, enabled beleaguered distance educators to compare their challenges as innovative but marginalized higher education colleagues and gain strength to return to their trenches. As Ian Mugridge explained, 'we huddled together for warmth'. Judith George's explanation for valuing a cohort of peers is based on a similar minority argument with the added element of having local supportive colleagues at home for the bad times at work:

> . . . minorities always cling together and feel solidarity. We were so embattled against the massed ranks of the other conventional universities. And also because, in a sense, I think we were all fairly embattled in our own particular situations in that we were all working desperately

hard and having to juggle all kinds of commitments – families, life and work.

Donald McDonell, as a critical thinker and technology pioneer, regarded conferences as useful for their comparison functions: 'I don't know if I was influenced as much as supported or backed up by what I saw others doing.'

Within institutions, the creation of effective materials and courses has depended on respectful and effective relationships between distance educators and university faculty. Colin Yerbury, for example, insisted on valuing the instructor's autonomy in decision-making about the course delivery. His 'participatory approach' was based on leading faculty members through voluntary change and professional development 'on their own terms', being a 'silent partner' with them for their professional development. Sometimes, though, it should be noted, Colin's relationship-building with university peers was guided by discreet forms of *quid pro quo* with academic departments and strategic use of the 'money buys support' guideline. Fred Lockwood learned that critical feedback to professors-as-authors from course teams creates less defensiveness when tempered with verbally graceful and constructive, easily applicable suggestions. Colin Latchem, half a geographical world away, followed similar respect-, growth- and capacity-enhancing principles as he guided professors and lecturers:

> . . . our best work was in finding out the good things that were going on, or in people's minds, and then reinforcing these . . . helping staff with projects and programmes, setting up systems and networks that helped to identify and develop knowledge and skills in the teaching staff that could then be passed onto others . . . creating the climate, conditions and work patterns for continuous improvement.

Terry Gibson always valued the not-always recognized roles of librarians in effective distance mode delivery because, in part, their view was wider and their skills additive:

> . . . they bring a lot of insight in terms of the whole learning process, the environment in which the learning takes place, and recognizing that there's a whole lot of learning that takes place outside of the very specific environment that you might have created around the course.

Teamwork, arguably a theme so far, is specifically valued by Uli Bernath, especially for its power in difficult times: 'A team that is depending on weather changes is not a good team. The team must be able to survive crises.' Uli's competitive sports experience taught him to transfer certain learnings into his setting up and managing a distance education operation at a German university under somewhat uncertain conditions: attend to and maximize the ever-changing contextual dynamics; persevere; maintain 'constant development'. Most importantly, 'never give up . . . There is always a new chance after a disaster.'

Intrapersonal reflections

During the interviews, some introspective reflections emerged. Often said quickly and *en passant*, these frank comments appear to reflect people who valued and sustained their own self-agency and awareness of personal thinking styles.

Regarding self-agency, various participants focused on being ready for handling and creating effective action themselves. Judith George and a peer used the principle of running ahead of new developments by doing their own experimentation in order to gain proactive, conceptual power when the need arose for informed debate about the innovations. Louise Moran '[liked] making things happen' and Tony Bates saw himself as 'very output oriented'. A 'catalyst' for others' action is how an ex-chemistry teacher saw himself making things happen in OUUK course design teams or staff development workshops or book preparation. Without such catalyzing, he argued, nothing would have happened. After many reactions and results, however, the catalyst becomes 'tainted . . . and loses its effectiveness, and it's got to be refreshed'; a situation which caused the catalyzing Fred Lockwood a most hearty chuckle during the interview. Lee Taylor's skill in taking an undeveloped but high-potential idea and gathering the resources to 'take it forward' relates perhaps to the catalyzing metaphor; she brought her personal stimulants of 'passion and a glimpse of something that could develop'. Surrounding her activity was often a sense of excitement, felt as an energy to build the developing ideas into something more concrete. Janet Jenkins referred to her consultant's guiding value of proactively analysing all the factors in a complex situation with 'independence of mind and . . . confidence'. She valued being very honest about 'standing by [her] own principles', even if it meant finding a way to state tactfully but unambiguously her judgement that a course of action proposed by a client could not work.

Consider this level of knowledge of 'self' held by Shona Butterfield:

> I've always understood myself in terms of having options and taking responsibility for the choices that I will make, and recognizing there are consequences for those. So I find it quite difficult when people have a totally different orientation from that – where they think it's some external force that actually determines what they will do.

Such an internal locus of control does not preclude her seeking help for learning, but the ultimate impact of the help may reach beyond her learning goals to a broader appreciation of the 'person' who gives appropriate help:

> *Shona:*   . . . that's pretty strong in my life: 'help me learn.' I'm always wanting to do something new, and 'help me learn' how do to that.
>
> *Liz:*   It seems to relate back to your earlier two themes of self-agency and self-responsibility.
>
> *Shona:*   Yes. [pause] Another theme would be 'It was not what you

taught me that I learnt so well while we walked side by side: it was who you were that stayed with me long after our ways did divide.' I can't think who wrote it, but I've always remembered it.

Regarding awareness of thinking style preferences to guide action, several participants remarked on their needs and habits. After Lee Taylor discussed her approaches to initiating change (including 'raising [her] head above the parapet' to better scan the territory) and managing its politics, she, like Janet Poley, ventured into reflecting on the value of using her intuitive thinking strength and balancing it with concrete and debatable evidence before considering appropriate solutions. When asked an impromptu question about her own evidence for being a reflective practitioner, her answer came carefully:

> . . . pause, time out . . . a conscious effort to consider what pattern has emerged from the activity of one's being, whether knee-deep or neck-deep or over-your-head in, and draw out understandable strands from that. Now sometimes . . . I would break that in terms of a set of theories, one or two that I use constantly.

When asked soon afterwards for a metaphor that might capture how she thinks in professional settings, she chose the kaleidoscope to explain her preferences for actively seeking patterns among complex and often inchoate ideas:

> . . . much of the time the kaleidoscope end is turning and actually choosing to stop it at various points and adjust: [asking] 'Is that a more pleasing pattern? Is it a pattern that resonates with what I think it should or could be?'. . . sometimes you think you see patterns that you wouldn't necessarily have thought of yourself.

Janet Poley's conceptual, dynamic thinking patterns are felt before she can find the words to describe them. Then her analyses find direction: 'I've got to see the relationships, the boundaries, how this is going to impact that.' Her earlier TV production experience helped her become highly integrative in her thinking, with a very strong intuitive capacity to foresee likely outcomes. She experiences her lateral thinking and her work in systems theory as complementary.

The second narrative as an ending

After so many guiding ideas and principles centred around equitable access to education, respect for and responsiveness to learners and their contexts, deliberative design and production of engaging learning materials, and supportive collegial relationships, it is time to close with the second narrative. It illuminates the respect where it counts most for the participants – in guiding their interactions with adult learners.

Raj Dhanarajan regarded the moment below as his proudest achievement, but we may consider it as evidence of his moral guidance:

> I was on the platform to lead the first congregation [graduation] of the Open Learning Institute in Hong Kong. And a person was wheeled in onto the platform to receive his scroll from the Governor of Hong Kong. As his wheelchair was being pushed across the stage, there was this little voice . . . saying, 'That's Daddy!' There was dead silence in the hall . . . I automatically stood up . . . [and] told myself 'It's all worth it.'

4

Managing technology: strategy, strengths and critique

Liz Burge

> ... some of the core lessons remain the same ... I hope some place there continues to be a focus on distance education teaching and learning; and the technology of the moment is secondary.
>
> (Terry Gibson)

Liz: What have you learned then about the adoption of new technologies?

Claire Matthewson: Old is no more dead than new is uncritically better. Out of context, they're value-neutral and not mutually exclusive.

Participants offered many and sometimes spirited comments, organized here into definitions and broad views, reflections on particular technologies, strategic implementation and thinking critically. You will note some links here to the chapter on lessons learned.

Definitions and broad views

The few participants who explained directly the concept of 'technology' saw it as a tool to achieve a process or reach a goal (as distinct from an organized body of specialist knowledge). Any intelligent application operates to extend effectiveness in communication and everyday tasks. Because the features of any technology act as strengths and weaknesses, it is the educator's challenge to identify and assess their potential impacts during the stages of institutional adoption, curriculum design and teaching implementation. Informed technology application is a defining attribute of effective distance education. Such application mediates human relationships between a learner and her or his tutor and course colleagues. It also mediates cognitive relationships between a learner and his or her material resources. That mediation should function transparently, i.e., the technology becomes invisible in the processes of learning and teaching.

Such transparency results from deliberate and sustained attention to detail. The smallest operational details and attention to defined standards become crucial if one is to avoid trouble; for example, 'when the picture fails, people talk. When the audio fails, people walk' (Janet Poley). Detail is also a factor in the style of communication used for audio (radio and recorded forms) and print: despite the technological reach to large numbers of students across distances (broadcast style), the communication style has to be felt as 100 per cent personalized, enveloping the user in a private world with the speaker (narrowcast style). A final example of where detail is significant lies in course content: it has to be particularized and tested for local application via analyses that fit learners' interests and life contexts.

Each participant who responded values a balanced and critical mindset toward each technology type. Acknowledging that each technology, old as well as new, carries its own particular functions and features, participants generally held an open mind toward exploring and evaluating the potential of emerging technologies without needing to uncritically and instantly adopt. Citing current examples of overly complicated design of technologies, Tony Bates, like others, stressed two points: while technology changes, the fundamental processes of learning do not, and that 'new technology is not always better than old technology. So it makes no sense to throw away what we do know and pretend everything is new.' Being very practical, John Thomas's agreement comes from his designs for audio/radio technology: 'just because it is old and cheap and accessible, don't ignore it'.

Particular technologies

Participants' reflections here relate most to audio (mostly educational radio with back-up print and discussions), broadcast television, print, online, with a few notes on 'learning objects'. Generally, the contexts are higher education, but several include vocational and international development settings (e.g., World Bank or country-funded projects) for adults learning literacy and pre-university courses.

Audio formats, especially radio, demand quality preparation and preferably professional levels of production. Audio cassettes, live telephonic conferencing (audio and video forms) and internet-based audio formats, if designed well, may also carry value: for their affective impact; for their appropriateness to learners who acquire and process information auditorially (a learning style issue); for their capacity to represent the sounds of the real world and the opinions of experts; for their mediation in attempting replication of face-to-face interaction; for their reduction or lack of sensory or visual clutter; and for their planned 'fit' with supportive print learning materials. One audio expert claimed that he 'could teach you how to take a motorcycle engine apart and put it together again using audio, because you can be looking at the pictures while I, as the teacher, talk to you' (John Thomas). When produced for asynchronous use, a tape recording or an internet-available sound clip gives the learner control over its timing and frequency of use. Tony Dodds's experience with radio learning groups and mass adult learning campaigns led to his recognition of radio's extension value: 'putting teaching into places where the teacher couldn't reach'. Claire Matthewson added another benefit for radio, based on challenging climatic conditions: print is affected by salty air, for example, but radio is not, and everyone has a radio – even if they have no telephone or electric light. Janet Poley's experience with radio convinced her of the value of audio formats, especially telephone-based discussions, because that technology is so ubiquitous. Evaluation of audio formats in use is useful but not easy, especially when the audio is seamlessly integrated with other course media.

Programming for broadcast educational television, one of Naomi (Sargant) McIntosh's specialties, helped her better understand how the design of the programmes must account for the key impact of television. It is 'intuitive; [it] is quite emotional and you really have to understand that. You can't just sit there and be analytical and say "stop that". The piece has to work intuitively . . . once the narrative stops and doesn't work, you lose people's attention.' In pioneering educational programming for Channel 4 in the UK, she learnt that every educational television programme must have an expressed purpose and clear stimulus, using various programme formats. Despite the power of television to attract and hold viewers' attention ('otherwise people wouldn't spend millions on television advertising campaigns'), Naomi regrets the fall from fashion of this medium in education. Like Naomi, Tom Prebble followed the principle of 'horses for courses' (media tailored to client needs) and knows that well-designed educational television may be 'brilliant' for some purposes, but is high in fixed cost (although low in variable cost) and needs to show evidence of high-volume audiences.

Well-designed print as a mediating technology for learning and teaching has been a foundation technology in distance education for approximately 150 years. It is still valued. Basically, any print format should engage the learner cognitively and affectively, using various in-text verbal and visual strategies to guide reading and activities. Attention to clear writing and perceptually effective layout is considered essential by participants. Michael Lambert recalled, with respect, an early example of what today we call 'granularity' or 'reusable learning objects'. Thirty-something years ago each one was called a Single Lesson Assignment Booklet (SLAB), with a maximum of 30 pages: 'It was plug and play anywhere you wanted.'

Reflections about online environments generally seemed based on a blend of qualified opportunity and a need for potential impact evaluations before any large-scale adoption. Ronnie Carr's stance is typical of many comments, showing balanced approaches to optimizing the potential of the technology in learning and teaching terms: 'I find the experience of online teaching and learning interesting. I see myself as somewhere in the middle – not an evangelist and not a Neanderthal . . . I don't really see the point of putting courses online in the same form as the printed versions – you are simply passing the print costs to students and you're not using the potential of the medium.' Dan Granger's assessment that online learning may provide a 'rich and powerful learning medium' was echoed by some others. Despite decades of experience with various technologies, Daryl Nation believes that we still need 'a broader understanding' of how all technologies may better assist learning. Using writing as one example of an enduring and powerful technology, he argues for developing appropriate academic conventions for today's web-based 'writing', as was done for earlier forms of writing production by hand, typewriter and word processor.

Dominique Abrioux, Shona Butterfield, Ros Morpeth and Bernd Schach-stiek, as institutional leaders, spoke positively of harnessing the power of computing for more effective production and revision of course materials, efficient administration of records systems and speedy, individualized, client-impressing service responsiveness: 'For me, online is synonymous with ser-vice. It requires you to meet demands. You have to focus much more on service in delivering online than you do in delivering traditional distance education . . . time delays are things of the past' (Dominique Abrioux). As leader of a large education company helping many thousands of adult learn-ers, Bernd Schachstiek regarded the online context as just one tool in a mix of media formats: 'It's not *the* tool' [his emphasis] because people present greatly differing styles in learning.'

Several participants used a critical, context-assessing view towards online learner behaviour, and especially for the issue of learners remaining cogni-tively and affectively engaged. Gail Crawford, for example, confessed to being a 'practical pragmatist' as she lived through the hyperbole of new technologies and technology-driven thinking. Knowing that there 'is usually more than one way to do things' and that not all students can or want to read course resources in online formats, she knows that while an online context may attract students to a course, such attraction will not last, nor help learning much, if those students do not 'actively engage in the learning processes'. She also accepts a key limitation to her effectiveness as an online tutor: despite her best facilitation strategies, ultimately the course con-ferencing 'will only be as good or as bad as the participants in it'. Looking at engagement in terms of how learners use higher order thinking skills to synthesize and test the applicability of new information for local contexts, Chère Gibson learned that her online teaching style created the demand to be 'supportive but not dominant'.

Maggie Coats's very cautious approaches to online work relate to her pref-erences in information processing, her need for task efficiency (it is often quicker for her to pick up the phone) and her distrust, so far, in any beliefs that the face-to-face 'encounter' for teaching and for staff development can be replaced effectively by online contexts. The concept of effectiveness in teaching and learning needs more explication, in her opinion, since 'it's very difficult to get people to sit down and talk about teaching and learning when they're technology-driven'. Here is another caution from a now part-time tutor of graduate studies: '. . . talking to students online breeds a curious kind of intimacy that you don't often get in classrooms. Many of the students that I have . . . end the semester by my knowing more about them then I would know about classroom students, and their knowing more about me. I don't find it surprising any more, but I did at the beginning. And I think that is probably good' (Ian Mugridge).

The few who referred to the development of reusable learning objects (RLOs) mostly offered comments of hesitation, essentially based on two factors they recognize from their preliminary thinking about RLOs. The first is individual ownership of and pride in such intellectual property (the 'not invented here' syndrome that would block RLO exchange). The second factor is the unexplored demands on time and effort expected in organizing/cataloguing the detail, especially for personal needs. While Gary Miller thinks that, in general, RLOs are 'an idea whose time has come', Terry Gibson expects that the application of RLOs will be slow and a 'struggle' because of the need to identify the highest quality resources and the difficulty in other academics accepting or sharing them. Tom Prebble knows of similar acceptance problems: 'Why would university teachers, who considered themselves good teachers already, want to purchase an RLO in their field and produced by a stranger?' Greville Rumble's experimentation with making RLOs for his online teaching (in itself an increase in teaching workload) indicates that attempts at creating banked answers to student questions are not efficient. He suggests more concrete and practical analyses of RLOs by their current promoters: 'Think about it – the cataloguing, the search time, the fact that reusing objects for questions with different nuances loses something for the student and for the tutor. We all recycle our own material to a degree. But as a kind of way of solving the cost and time issues in tutoring, it doesn't ring true to me.'

Strategic implementation

The participants reflections on how best to implement technologies centred on knowing learners' contexts, assessing access, promoting effective teaching and maintaining effective infrastructures.

Sustaining a focus on learners involves giving them technology options, maintaining print technology, following the everyday contexts of learners, and accepting that learners will make their own choices regardless of what educators prescribe.

Giving technology options is not easy to achieve. Louise Moran's experience revealed two difficulties in trying to embed a mix of technologies in a course: one is the expected cost and the other is the enforced need to make tough choices when not every idiosyncratic learning style can be accommodated by its optimum mediating technology. Gail Crawford echoes the cost issue in arguing for a mix of old and new technologies, especially in developing countries where operational reliability and low cost technology provision (e.g. pencils or paper) may be overriding issues. Shona Butterfield explained how the Open Polytechnic in New Zealand offered real-time technologies (audioconferencing, audio-graphic, videoconferencing) but discovered that what many students really needed was asynchronous technology. Overall, their guiding principle became 'to keep the core [technology requirements] as open as we possibly could'.

Many participant comments stressed the continuing value of print materials for multi-format delivery of key course content, rather than dropping 'long reams of text' (Judith Fage) into online software for students to download and print off. Colin Yerbury added another point to the argument for mixes of technology: the lack of quality control at the student's printer leading to a possible 'loss of structural design' of the original text layout. He knows that faculty teachers understand the value of print but there is the ever-present 'danger' from senior administrators' focus on cost efficiency and productivity; not to mention their lack of understanding about the needs for system and human supports, i.e. the 'under-ware behind the delivery of a course'. Echoing Maggie Coats's earlier comments about human contact and effective use of time, Judith Fage believes that our needs for contiguous (face-to-face) and synchronous (real-time) contact will not disappear ('you still can't have a meal and a drink over the phone or via the computer').

Evidence of consistent use of everyday contexts and needs of learners as the base for planning flexible learning and teaching, 'as opposed to inflexibility where you say "distance education is computers, isn't it?" ' would lead Janet Jenkins to recognize a 'common sense' approach to technology implementation. Gail Crawford thinks similarly: she argues that decision-making about 'decreeing' any institutional move to electronic technology must consider 'the learner and the circumstances'. Bernd Schachstiek's staff made decisions based on the micro-detail of their learners' everyday life, such as when and where their learners could reasonably get time for studying (on public transportation going to work) and which technologies may be feasible for potential learners: 'What kind of technology do they really use and accept?' Michael Lambert quickly learned that learners need time-convenience scheduling of courses, so to keep 'market share' in course offerings, institutions are wise if they limit time-fixed, face-to-face activities.

Learners too will make their own choices about when, where and why they use any technology, despite teachers' intentions or planners' assumptions. Several participants noted how some of their students avoid online studying at night because they have to sit at a workplace computer all day. John Thomas's experience with audio and radio, for example, taught him how learners will make choices based on their own needs despite his best design and production intentions: 'in the end they will take what they want from it and use it in the way that suits them'. Publicly available communication centres (telecentres) may help some learners who need discretion when they seek help, as Colin Latchem discovered: 'farmers' wives who wouldn't even dare admit to their husbands that they were taking a distance education course because they were fearful of what would happen if they did. At least when they go into . . . one of these telecentres, they can talk to someone.'

Assessing access

Equitable access to appropriate mediating technologies is generally viewed in terms of its hindrances. The lack of a reliable technological infrastructure in a country, inadequate financial resources of the learners to buy a computer and pay for the ongoing communications charges, and the impacts of work and other life roles on learners' resources for learning are some examples of hindrances.

While she acknowledges the 'exciting blue skies' offered by new online technology, for example, Janet Jenkins is just one participant who has learned not to make any assumptions about easy and reliable access to computer technology, even though a learner may claim that a computer is accessible. Ronnie Carr's context here is the high-density living in Hong Kong: 'If you have a computer in a small cramped flat . . . which you share with your family, are you really going to be able to use it whenever you want or need to?' Claire Matthewson knows that the portability and tactility of print, not to mention as a cost effective alternative to downloading online texts, still carry fitness for purpose for many of her students who 'still like . . . to take a book to read in bed or sitting by the river, [or] on the train'. Tony Dodds's experience in Namibia leads him to ask tough questions about local infrastructure when determining technology decisions:

> If 5 per cent of [the middle-class, professional career] students have access to [computer] technology, why are we spending all our time talking about the technology rather than about the things that they do have access to? Or . . . saying 'how can we make that technology available and sustained?'

Half a world away, in the USA, Dan Granger was concerned about the level of institutional awareness of the issue of equitable access to technology-mediated courses: 'We are creating yet another separation – the technology haves and have-nots – [and it] is pretty appalling. We seem to have lost the need to reach out and to provide truly accessible learning opportunities to new populations.' Like several other participants, Janet Jenkins sees how extensive online use tends to 'download' more costs onto learners, especially when learners do not receive the necessary text materials as separate print packages.

Promoting effective teaching

Since some technology-related teaching issues are reported above, this section adds a few final comments on what Terry Gibson terms part of the 'human infrastructure' factor. Discussion here was centred around course design and teaching excellence and high levels of persuasive skill and tact in working with academics.

Fashionable technology will not rescue an inherently poor course design. Its uniform application may also reduce learning outcomes and learner satisfaction. Colin Latchem's metaphorical question graphically represents this issue of technology-driven thinking: 'Are you sure you're not putting a go-fast stripe on a clapped out old banger [dilapidated car]?' When design efforts do not succeed in learning terms, what Colin terms a 'bum steer [animal unfit for purpose]' is born: a failure of appropriate teaching resulting from 'putting too much faith into technologies and too much [burden] on the teacher. Like being a carpenter and only going out with a hammer or a saw, where [instead] you'd need a screwdriver and a whole lot of other [tools].' Chère Gibson met a 'bum steer' when she encountered a misuse of videoconferencing in a poetry course. Not only was its use financially unsustainable, but the use of the visual capacity of the technology undermined what should have been happening in the learners' heads: 'If you give me a visual [relating to] a poem, I may have a different visual; and you have ruined my imagination by sticking your [disruptive] visual in my way.' Chère therefore values 'low technology', defined as non-duplicative, non-intrusive and never destructive of the learner's power to respond independently to stimuli and create new meaning. Tony Bates once faced a similar experience with the mindsets of television production designers. They focused on designing and building a brilliantly imaginative and complex working model to illustrate a physics principle, only to be confronted and surprised later by evidence that viewers could not understand what they should have learned from that brilliant model. Terry Gibson summed up this seductive impact of 'shiny' new technology as being 'enamoured with special effects and [getting] sidetracked from your initial learning objectives'.

Working with academics is generally seen as innovation by stealth and helping them avoid seduction-by-technology. Colin Latchem recognized a transference potential when academics teaching in distance modes, i.e. using specially prepared learning materials and some mediating technologies, begin to use the materials and technologies in their face-to-face classes, thus bringing 'cost [and] educational benefits'. And if the academic had also learned additional generic skills for managing high-level scholarly discussions among students, even better for transfer to conventional classrooms. The generic skills include helping learners to develop confidence in using the technology, to feel academically and socially engaged with peers, and to use silence as a constructive thinking element. But first, all that learning for the academic has to occur. It is best facilitated by a discreet and patient distance education specialist or instructional designer or staff developer who knows how to avoid any perceived loss of status by the academic.

One strategy used by some participants is to hide the real reason for the training session. Here is one example from Claire Matthewson:

> We had to be very careful . . . university academics think they already
> know how to teach and they don't like being told or advised that they

might do things in other ways … The training sessions that we would regularly run … looked like technical workshops, but were much more. They always included examples of best [teaching] practice and interaction between staff and students.

Even when the distance mode teaching adviser is also a professor with expertise in his or her own discipline, time was needed for such skill development, as Donald McDonell noted: 'I can't manipulate the [professors] very much. I can't take a poor prof and turn them into a good prof overnight.' Patience is a virtue here also because busy academics need time to assess the potential and fit of any new technology and develop the appropriate skills for using it. Colin Latchem learned that 'generally speaking, technological change takes much longer than you think'.

Explaining the best practical teaching strategies is not the only challenge of anyone assisting in the provision of high-quality technology-mediated teaching. Terry Gibson is one participant who knows about the wider contextual challenge – how to help academics avoid being 'easily seduced by the glitter and glamour of technology' when surrounded by 'very creative, very enthusiastic technology people or graphic artists [who] may have lots of great ideas [and] can find lots of ways to spend time and spend money'. This complex issue of culture confrontations was explicated in terms of new technology meets traditional academic culture by Tom Prebble, who led some institution-wide interrogations of the issue:

> Could we use [online learning] with our old culture? Is it new wine into old bottles? … How are we going to embrace online learning? … And would we actually be doing a violence to the culture that's served us pretty well to date? Are we essentially telling a thousand academics, 'Okay, you can go and do what you like in these other modes, like paper-based and campus-based, or teleconferencing, but if you want to use the online medium, then you come to mother and mother will tell you what's good for you, and you'll like it!' That would be such a source of dislocation in this place, we didn't want to do it.

Maintaining effective infrastructures means in essence 'getting the system right' (Patrick Guiton) or 'keeping the trains running' (Terry Gibson). Again, attention is due to even the smallest components in each system, as in the proverb 'a chain is only as strong as its weakest link'. Here are a few examples.

At the classroom and teaching levels, several participants stressed that technical staff should not be allowed to control operations such as room layouts, networks, software choice or other decisions about teaching and learning technology applications. But they (the 'tekkies') should be in positions to provide extensive support so that each technology is transparent to its users and no undue distractions occur for the academic. Donald McDonell insisted on complete transparency, giving two examples from his work in teaching peers how to use new technologies. Don't allow distraction-by-technology: 'Don't ask profs to touch anything. They walk into the room, they put their microphone on, or you put it on for them and adjust it properly, and let them [begin the class].' Knowing when to insist that a commercial technology needs modification and persisting until the change happens, even against initial resistance by technical personnel, needed his unwavering commitment to transparent use. Donald also learned to be strategic about which senior university colleagues he told about his innovations, especially in their earliest stages: '. . . make sure the higher administration knows [about trying a new technology]; but then . . . don't let all the layers of higher administration know'.

Teachers and students should not assume, however, that ease of technical operation correlates with easy (low-level) cognition. Terry Gibson argues that academics therefore need high levels of appropriate teaching skills and learners need the appropriate attitudes (as well as skills) for high levels of scholarly discussion.

For organization-level thinking, Patrick Guiton stressed that the origins of successful application do not lie in the latest fashionable technology itself but in how staff plan for and implement it for the most challenging recipients:

> There's nothing magic about online learning, any more than there was anything magic about satellite learning and video learning or anything else. You've got to get the systems right [i.e.] making sure that whatever teaching and learning structures you set up are done with the student in mind, starting with the most isolated student. If it'll work for that one, it should work for everybody.

Shona Butterfield also prioritized learners in technology system planning, and adds three other factors: the extent of relative value offered by each technology; critical thinking in general; and the key concept of 'readiness'. That last analytical lens appears to be so obvious as to defy explication, but its scope has to be deliberately broad, focusing on the technical capacity of the local community-based 'telecom infrastructure' as well as the learners' and the institutional staff's capacities for managing any new technology. Regarding how organizational capacity may influence the success of online innovations, Fred Lockwood had to manage the results of inadequate staff infrastructures at his second university; for example, overloaded help-desk and teaching advising operations, and 'quite a pedestrian – in the main – form of online learning'.

Gary Miller sees now a major change over three decades in the rationale for US organizational cooperation regarding new technologies. It has moved from expense-reducing cooperation for system-wide sharing of course/materials production and distribution to today's cooperation for sharing standards for internet use in higher education, marketing to the end-user and managing the 'institutional transformation that the internet caused'.

Thinking critically

Many of the reflections above show how participants questioned unspoken assumptions and challenged conventional wisdom. This section adds some final and overtly critical reflections about managing the hyperbole of early adopters and the stages of adoption.

Hyperbole is seen to be evident in some commercial marketing and educational literature. Hilary Perraton, for example, funnelled his extensive experience into a concise assessment: 'Watch out. Be sceptical. If you look at the literature of how television was going to transform education a generation ago and then look at literature about how e-learning is going to do it, it is the same sort of language. It wasn't true the first time, I doubt if it is true the second time.'

Having similarly extensive experience with various technologies, Colin Latchem, however, sees some progress in learning from past technology deficiencies:

> There was the audio-visual aids movement . . . programmed learning . . . teaching machines . . . multimedia (the first time round) . . . resource-based learning . . . resource centres . . . educational television . . . and all of these things were going to transform teaching and learning. And they were all found, in their various ways, to be deficient. I think what's happening now is that the lessons learned from these earlier experiences are slowly coming to light and being integrated.

Tom Prebble learned about the vulnerability factor when critical thinking is not applied. Leaders and administrators, especially early adopter types, do not always recognize marketing hyperbole, nor always resist copying another institution's decisions. So 'when you've got a good match, then put [in] the planning and get the investment: do it right. But don't buy a solution until you're absolutely sure it's a solution to *your* problem, rather than somebody else's problem.' Glen Farrell also managed what he named the 'bandwagon' effect. His way of interrogating the proposed adoption of a new technology meant investigating access, usability and cost issues. Cost, for him, operates at two levels. The cost of the technology itself 'is the easy bit'. The costs needed for student support and for course design activity are more difficult to manage and result generally in long-term system-wide expenses. So decision-making merits much pre-purchase analysis, especially as 'very few [conventional] universities set out to achieve economies of scale in their programmes'.

Managing the stages of technology adoption demands two tasks. The first is to limit the claims of apparent significance made by early adopters. The second is to be analytically independent, well prepared and patient enough to allow time for analysing the impacts and benefits of new technologies. While Tom Prebble looked for the early lessons he and his university colleagues learned, they were not his only source of information; later adopters also would contribute other lessons. Time was a factor for David Warr because it is needed for developing infrastructure stability (e.g. 'a reliable telephone system . . . available batteries') before educators plan uses for any new technology. Similarly, Greville Rumble knew the benefits of waiting. After the early pronouncements from conference speakers seen as taking 'leading edge' positions about a new technology, he would eventually read the analyses from some 'second generation' adopters. Using their more extensive practice, these writers were valued because they 'deepen the message and extend our understanding in a really useful way'. This quality of intellectual resource, however, is seen to be limited in the overall literature. There is also some 'really dangerous stuff [that] is opinion masquerading as sound policy advice'. Often missing, for Greville at least, 'is the stuff that queries the received wisdom on e-learning – that asks, if you like, whether this new emperor has any clothes on'.

When prior technologies have not been adequately assessed for their impact on learning, teaching and institutional operations, those trying to examine the potential of a new technology may discover multi-layered difficulties. Judith George did:

> it was too easy for the tekkies to rush and present [computer conferencing] as the solution to our problems – economical and effective in reaching all students. But because we hadn't worked out what the impact on the learning experience of the different media were, in a rigorous way, and at a level at which you could pose challenging questions to the people who were wanting to substitute computer contact for everything, we were not able to defend face-to-face contact or the use of other media. We were not able to pinpoint what particular learning outcomes a particular mode of contact was suited to [so] . . . We needed a pedagogy for this technology.

Living through a later decade of computer experience meant that Judith became involved with widespread adoption trials before the institution realized that there are some limits to wholesale acceptance of a single technology – 'coming back a way and realizing that not everything can be done electronically'. One legacy, however, remains. It is not seen by Judith as contributing to critical thinking about technology's relationship to learning because the primary focus of thinking is on the technology itself, not on the learning and teaching issues: 'A lot of IT staff development is about how to manage the software, not about how to manage the learning; and courses are totally online, with feedback from students which seems to be saying that this is causing serious difficulties.'

Two 'bookends' show the broad scope of reflections about technology implementation. Claire Matthewson points to current human- and resource-related limits of technology applications as potential solutions to educational problems: 'There are many distances out there [for which] technology is not the ultimate answer.' Tony Bates raises a regression issue, commonly known as 'old wine in new bottles', when adoptions of new technologies produce no innovations in teaching styles but reinforce less than effective old ones:

'The next wave [of changing technologies], which will probably be in three or four years' time, will be synchronous technologies. My worry there is that we will go back to doing lectures over the internet.'

Finally, two principles appear to integrate the reflections for this chapter. The first relates to the famous phrase from Wilbur Schramm (in *Big Media, Little Media*, 1974) quoted by Patrick Guiton. In essence, and despite all the alluring promises, there is no single super-technology that answers all the complex contextual questions across teaching and learning. The second principle is to maintain focus on the end user, especially the learners and their local contexts. However unpopular that stance may become, persist with it. Know when 'technology really does add value'. Know too a corollary from David Hawkridge: that what may be *feasible* to do with technologies may not be *desirable* to do.

5

Learning from experience:
hard-won lessons

Liz Burge

To respect, and to respond: these goals best thematically represent how participants identified many lessons learned experientially over their career. Respect is accorded to learners, to oneself as a professional and to professional colleagues. Responsiveness is applied to the processes of learning, teaching effectiveness, facilitative models of teaching and proactive design of quality learning resources. To respect and to respond is associated with the two other topic areas generating much learning – innovation management and institutional administration. Lessons learned specifically about the use of learning and teaching technologies nest in Chapter 4. This chapter ends with some indicators of the personal qualities needed for instigating or managing change, referring here to designing, implementing or revising distance modes of postsecondary education. Now, the details.

Respect

To respect learners is to recognize the embedded and embodied nature of learning. Embedded refers here to the positioning of learners inside their chosen or typical communities of interest and/or location which influence how those learners seek, construct, apply, evaluate new information and integrate the new knowledge into existing knowledge frameworks. Judith George explains:

> distance learning really grows within the communities – like a plant in a flowerbed – [so] don't just zap knowledge like a thunderbolt out of the blue to a person. A student is a person in a variety of contexts and the better that learning is meshed into the person's other contexts, the more effective it will be.

Embodiment refers here to how learning is integral to a learner's motivational, cognitive, affective, psychological and behavioural needs, histories, rewards and current actions. Patrick Guiton's experience, for example, of how adult university students show 'their motivation, intelligence and scarce time' is captured in this anecdote:

> The great respect I have for people's capacity to achieve things . . . a farmer's wife [living] a long way [from Perth] won the [Murdoch] University Medal. I went to visit her once and it took me a day to get there, eventually driving across a paddock to the station house. The student was there with a couple of preschool kids, her course materials scattered on the dining table. She's cooking lunch with one hand and directing communications for the local volunteer bush fire brigade with the other.

Others referred to their respect for students' accumulation of experiential and career knowledge: '. . . you can't be condescending to them . . . the people taking my course are probably smarter than I am, probably more accomplished than I am . . . Often, these students have something to give back to me as the tutor' (Michael Lambert). John Cowan learnt about how students' affective needs merit respectful attention, even though they may be couched in questions such as 'Am I finding this difficult because it's difficult, or am I finding it difficult because I'm stupid? How am I getting along relative to the others?' He construes affect as being 'enormously important' and '. . . partly about concerns and . . . partly also about values and how we handle them', rather than being about 'touchy feely things'. Learning problems need empathetic attention and respect for the impact of learners' life contexts. Bernd Schachstiek learned to use sensitivity as a criterion of quality services:

> know especially the learning problems; this is very important. It's not only that you are perfect in what you tell, you have to understand the problems the learner has during this process, and sometimes it has nothing to do with the subject. It has nothing to do with the language level you use. It has to do with kids around them, problems in the company, problems in the family . . . And somebody has just to feel that a little bit and to know how to help them.

Generation- and gender-related characteristics of learners have to be visibly respected. Here is one example.

> Young adults calling in [to the Open Polytechnic of New Zealand] for assistance didn't understand [the] language [of the older staff members], so we had to get some youth in there . . . This went right through to digital issues and there are real issues in there with your younger students who are far more digitally capable than many of the staff.
>
> (Shona Butterfield)

Respecting (but not necessarily valuing) assumptions about societally-induced gender roles means attending to how those assumptions might be reflected negatively in course content (through illustrations, language and concept examples) and discussions (through patterns of speech dominance or respecting others' life experience).

Respect means paying attention to relationship-building between learner and educator. The quality of such relationship-building, argued directly by two participants, but hinted at by others, should never be based on overt status differences, as in 'master, pupil' (Judith George) or 'a dictatorship' (Michael Lambert). Rather it has to be collaborative, always 'standing with the learners, getting to know them, getting to feel how they feel as much as you can and then encouraging them to say what they want, where they want to go next' (Judith George).

Adults have time-packed lives but do they want to give up anything for study time? Here several participants learned to respect what they knew could not be changed, despite their hopes to the contrary. For one participant, such respect referred to learners making their own choices: 'People have got so much jammed into their lives and are not very willing to give things up, as I discovered . . . But you have to give something up – back down a little bit in order to find the time for these degree programmes . . . The technology hasn't made it any faster' (Chère Gibson). Another participant learned about time in terms of flexibility needs: 'I believe young people are increasingly autodidactic . . . They don't have the patience, they are not going to listen to somebody. They want a different kind of learning and they want it any time, any place and they want it to be relevant. They find that e-learning can do that' (Dominique Abrioux).

Role-modelling all these ways of respecting learners, their contexts, styles and needs perhaps may best be summed up in Roger Mills's concept of a 'culture of care in learners and learning'.

Respect for self as professional

Learning here related to the capacity to transfer knowledge across conceptual boundaries, to valuing intuitive thinking, and willingness to take risks. Her reframing of the concept of creativity enabled Shona Butterfield to value idea-transference skills ('I took other people's ideas and applied them to our context'), to build them, and broaden her own capacity for creativity. Judith Fage learned to attend to 'what [her] common or ethical sense tells [her] is right or wrong . . .'; to trust her intuition; and interrogate her inner voice – to ask 'what is it that is making me so uneasy'? Gaining his own confidence in taking professional risks to stage and test innovations was a learning process for John Cowan: 'every time you take a risk you can go nearer and nearer to the edge of the cliff . . . without falling over'. He believed, however, in always having a 'safety net' for informed risk-taking in teaching, even for himself.

Confessing when he had 'failures' or had to 'muddle through or cut corners' was not an action preferred by Patrick Guiton, in his early days as a manager, because that would have created some private anxiety or even shown publicly his lack of formal training in management. Better, then, to close down internal, post-action reflection and present a good image

– 'shut off and just present a brag sheet'. That disclosure led to this exchange:

> *Liz:*   How would you recognize a reflective practitioner if you saw one?
>
> *Patrick:*   . . . it's got to be someone who's constantly thinking and look-
> ing to adapt, rather than just holding the line; constantly in
> dialogue with themselves and with others; and perhaps that's
> really what good management is about.

Later, Patrick returned to the question and added a criterion: 'the capacity and preparedness for self-criticism'.

Respect for colleagues

Effective collegial relationships within and beyond one's institution bring advantages as well as genuine recognition for the 'person' behind the professional presentation. The advantages include institutional and staff growth, networking for problem-solving, celebrating achievements, gaining greater confidence in oneself, knowing outside-institution trends and gaining increased trust of workplace staff. Above all are teamwork and the role-modelling of, in Raj Dhanarajan's phrase, 'people as principal asset'. Michael Lambert, for example 'learned not to take excessive pride about anything that I personally did . . . I cannot lay claim that I – alone – ever wrote a course or developed a programme. I learned early on that it is a team approach that works the best.' Leading course development teams at the Open University helped Fred Lockwood into a conversion of sorts. Rather than giving tough assessments of an academic's course draft, he converted his evaluations into opportunities for the academic to burnish her or his writing and reputation and feel free to disagree, thus avoiding defensive and dysfunctional reactions. John Cowan learned that if he trusted in and supported the growth of his students and staff to 'be the best that they could be', his gains were immense – 'a harvest ten times what I deserved'. Ros Morpeth was quite deliberate in connecting to international and national colleagues, finding the results 'absolutely incredibly valuable'. Showing respect through her priority for staff development activity (even when budgets were tight) and celebrations with staff, and students, were important for Judith Fage.

Responding

Responding to what is worthy of respect calls for a consistent and primary focus on learning and teaching. That means a secondary focus on technology. However 'clever' it is, technology is 'no replacement for good learning designs. The design of the learning is generic across all technology' (Ros Morpeth). Hear another view:

...you must develop programmes ... faculty are important, brains are important, concepts are important, teacher/learner relations are important. And then if you think technology helps these important players in the field to achieve their goals ... then apply technology; but don't start with [it].

(Uli Bernath)

Learning and teaching lessons are grounded in knowing the processes of learning and providing effective and holistic teaching and guidance. The processes of learning are complex and interlinked with personal growth and current life experience, as Judith George explained:

[adults] have a huge range of learning experiences as schemas or arenas in which they have an identity. Now in social-psychological terms, the better these are integrated the more a person can mature ... as they develop into new areas of learning, this learning sticks; and they get the most out of it if it makes sense in ways other than just on its own terms.

Deliberative experiential enquiry helps Gary Miller avoid an unquestioning reliance on 'folk wisdom' and instead unravel intentions and impacts behind the actions of professional practice: 'Intellectual rigour', understanding learning from the student's perspective and consistently honouring that perspective are prerequisites to 'doing this stuff right', because, as he added, 'the technology will change, the faculty we work with will change, the institutional setting will change, but still we are always trying to achieve change in a student'.

Teaching effectiveness covers being formally qualified in teaching (not just in one's discipline), being monitored appropriately, using proactive design for producing quality learning resources, adopting facilitative (not transmissive) models of teaching, and using proactive staff to ensure effective in-course learning experiences. All in all, the need to give 'due care and attention' to any teaching model or strategy (Gail Crawford) was echoed by many participants.

Being qualified in how to teach in universities and having quality-minded managers knowing about actual teaching behaviours was an important lesson for Louise Moran:

[teachers] should go through a formal process of learning about curriculum design and curriculum development, about how students learn, about assessment, about the whole panoply of pedagogy. I could see such learning happening among academics in distance education more palpably than in the face-to-face environments because [the distance mode teachers] struggle a great deal when they are confronted with using different technologies to mediate the communication of information, negotiation of meaning and assessment of the outcomes. The quality of the course materials is directly related to the capacity that the author has to think through the design of them; and people need to learn how to do it.

Preparation for teaching is not enough, however; what happens during the course to maintain quality? In Judith Fage's experience, being monitored while working with learners and their materials is a delicate issue for the course teacher (usually called tutor) as well as the administrators:

> There isn't any substitute for proper performance management of teaching staff. If you fail to implement that, it will always catch up with you in the end and cause you more problems than you would ever have had if you had properly managed it. So that was a hard lesson to learn but it's an essential one. Again, it's all to do with teachers wanting and feeling they have a right to a lot of autonomy, but ... it's still very difficult to tell a teacher that they are not doing their job properly.

Proactive design of quality learning resources

Working determinedly toward quality as an end in itself ran through many narratives and comments. Not just for the students' sakes but also because quality outcomes and products would influence public attitudes to distance education in general. Course design teams, however small, as long as they incorporated a range of skills in content and learning design, acted to maintain quality standards as well as gain greater creativity. Many participants learned never to assume that adults abandoned their expectations of service quality as soon as they became a student. Michael Lambert, who has seen 'everything – the good, the bad and the ugly' in his formal evaluations of postsecondary programme designs, learned about when quality should be considered: 'Our learners ... can sense what quality in learning should be. Maybe they can't define it, but they know when they are taking a well-crafted programme, and it ... will keep them studying ... Thus I learned that you had to build the quality *into* the programme, not tack it on later.' Ian Mugridge and his workplace colleagues took seriously the principle of quality assurance and located it in everyday action: 'we just called it doing your job properly'. Course writers, tutors and advisers had to be subject to quality standards: they were monitored, and failure to meet deadlines for marking assignments or provide helpful written comments would lead to the miscreants becoming 'toast'.

The deliberative – thoughtful, informed, and tested – design of learning was another aspect. Shona Butterfield's reflection speaks for many others:

> good open distance learning has always had at its core whatever you can bring to bear that will help those students learn, and has understood the need to *design* a learning experience; that it just isn't serendipitous ... you support that learner to learn. And that's much more than simply putting content across.

The value of specified, educator-desired learning outcomes was acknowledged by Maggie Coats: 'Properly handled [they] are an aid to good design and good delivery . . . as long as we're not too tick-boxy or knee-jerking, you know'. Experience in supervising the design and evaluation of course materials lay behind David Hawkridge's key lessons here:

> keep courses shorter . . . attend to the means of assessment very early on and begin the debate about what the student has to do for whatever and get past the looking for hidden curricula . . . do developmental testing on the materials . . . [and functionally integrate all the media for the course].

Two other design factors – scheduling and pacing – prompted some lessons: 'Since the major reason for using distance modes to gain postsecondary qualifications is convenience and minimized disruption of life schedules, then any market-share-minded educator will minimize the number of scheduled synchronous or real-time discussions' (Michael Lambert). Yet that does not mean leaving students in 'free form' altogether. When distance modes are used in conventional universities, the pacing that is based on the deadlines of the traditional university year also acts as a 'good motivator' (Patrick Guiton).

Promoting facilitative, not transmissive, models of teaching

Several participants focused in part on learning about what Judith George might call the 'anti-zap' model, and I call an 'informed companion' stance for the academic person (often called a tutor) who works with the distance mode learner. This tutor does not need to 'transmit' content because it already has been designed and set out in learning resources or via links given to web-based caches. But she or he does need a clear idea of why, when, and how they intervene in the learner's activity in order to be cognitively and affectively supportive. Many participants had learned about the importance of flexible and informed 'tutors', 'tutoring', and 'facilitating'. Maggie Coats strengthened her conviction about the role of the tutor *vis-à-vis* the role of the pre-prepared course materials. Any academic colleagues assuming that the course materials were the 'real' teacher, and that 'traditionally [Open University (OUUK)] tutors "don't teach" ', would provoke her clarification: 'Well, excuse me. Every moment of every interaction I had with my students was about teaching.' Even now, with today's fast access to huge amounts of information, and compared to the 1970s and 1980s OUUK policy of total provision 'in a box', the tutor still carries an essential role: 'now with the library, with electronic resources, you can open up so many possibilities to students. But that in turn needs an awful lot of support and teaching to enable students to actually use those sources for learning.' David Hawkridge characterized the best interactions with learners as 'a conversation; it's much more about "well, this is what I think; what do you think?" . . . about trying to raise in them that critical experience'. Not inducing learner-dependency behaviours was a lesson for Bernd Schachstiek and his teaching staff: 'We learned . . . that certain kinds of teachers did not work for us, because they act more like parents instead of helping somebody to try to find his or her own way. The Nightingale complex, as we call it, is not good for business. You should care for somebody, but in a sense [make them] fit to do it by [themselves]. It's really supporting people, but not taking them by the hand and leading them somewhere.'

Conducting the tutorial role is not always comfortable, not the least because of learning style differences among and between learners and tutor. It is too easy to impose one's own individualized set of learning style preferences on the students, as Janet Poley (as tutor) found out: '. . . think about how different people approached learning and that you have a variety of differences in learning styles and trying to help people learn . . . I should be pushed out of shape and work within *their* learning style or their way of wanting to work.'

When facilitation deliberately promotes meta-learning skill development in learners, i.e., moving to high levels of thinking and increasing writing and reading skills, the rewards may be high. Colin Yerbury likened such 'human capacity' development as a duty to mentor as well as the duty to grade assignments.

Maggie Coats 'discovered' the implications of attending to the metacognitive aspects, as in 'learning how to learn', and realized that the focus of the learning has to stay on the learner. She, as the teacher, 'can only go so far' in helping the learner. Consider John Cowan's related reflection: 'if you put a commitment of time into helping people to make judgements, to be analytical, to think about how they go about being creative, to think about how they interrelate with other people in a group, then you've got a tremendous payoff in terms of the associated learning'. As did Shona Butterfield, Judith George reinforced the importance of creating a holistic, total experience for an individual which will probably, almost necessarily, involve them reflecting about who they are as the starting point, in terms of knowledge, but also values and attitudes. '. . . the most important levels on the cognitive taxonomy are critical evaluation, synthesis, and analysis. And to practice that and to develop it you need to be thinking in terms of connections, mapping what you know already onto what is new.'

The importance of interpersonal communication applied to learner–learner interactions as well as learner–tutor interactions, and it is, in Tony Dodds's experience, 'crucial' to build it in from the very beginnings of a course design.

Innovation management

Here, and in institutional administration matters, the (often concisely stated) lessons were couched in terms of advice or operational principles. They follow, in no order of priority.

- Ensure that change is not gratuitous or merely following fashion.
- Persevering against lack of interest or ignorance takes conscious effort. Bernd Schachstiek surely would agree with Tom Prebble's lesson here: 'give an issue attention, passion and persistence . . . you can't expect an idea to sell itself'. 'Look for new possibilities in high-risk situations' (Lee Taylor). Louise Moran learned the need to 'orient your organization [to make change] even though it's going against the acceptable norms. You have to be willing to take risks along those lines.'
- Reliance on knowledge and cognition for persuasion arguments is not enough: 'being right never wins the day', as Dan Granger learned. He had to attend to his allies' emotions-based reactions: 'Even for a Walter Perry or Ernest Boyer, it's the affect – the way people take notions into their own sense of self – that makes things work.'
- Be realistic and limit the scope of innovation in distance education to schools and colleges within universities; not the whole university, 'because [that is not] going to happen' (Terry Gibson).
- Have allies. Know them. Know the opposition. Preferred allies are institutional 'champions' (Claire Matthewson, Glen Farrell); 'leadership – charismatic individuals – unsung heroes' (Janet Jenkins); 'powerful, advising, supportive but also fearless critics of one's arguments' (Lee Taylor); 'community and business leaders' (Raj Dhanarajan); 'faculty members' (Colin Yerbury); and staff in general may become allies. Echoed by several others was Uli Bernath's learning that support from the very top levels of the university is essential, especially if a separate administrative centre for distance education activity is planned, because if such support is lacking, 'your base is very fragile . . . [most] professors will not support [it] in a conventional environment. Why should they? It's not attractive because eight out of ten professors love the face-to-face, campus-based socialization of students.'
- Never become separated from potential allies' or current clients' expectations and needs.
- In developing arguments for change, be evidence-based. Always show that distance mode 'actually can have some value – it does work' (Janet Jenkins). Balance such analytical thinking with strongly intuitive thinking, but also be sure to 'present the business case'. Lee Taylor learned not to accept arguments about lack of money for innovation and therefore would develop a convincing, fiscal argument for success. One of Judith Fage's learnings also faces the hard realities of institutional politics: 'Try to counter ideology with evidence rather than counter-ideology.'
- Consider teaching innovation by stealth and by transfer of existing knowledge to new contexts. Use a 'horse' if necessary: 'You put the Trojan Horse out into the academic compound, and all these distance educators would hop out and start converting everybody. [That is, use] distance education as a mechanism for developing flexible learning strategies or online approaches [because] in successful distance education programmes you had all the elements needed to develop [flexible or online

learning] . . . I [heard] this [Trojan analogy] from someone at the Open University [UK]' (Brian Kenworthy).

- Anticipate the impacts of change on students and staff: 'Even if [change] is necessary, I think it has to be done with the utmost sensitivity to what it does to the human being' (Raj Dhanarajan).
- 'When rank and file staff own an innovative project and later its results, and if the leaders are seen to be in support, the chances of success are magnified. The best change happens when the people who propose change believe in it and can argue well toward an informed decision, and when staff affected by the change can discuss, evaluate, and own it. No one feels manipulated by ephemeral arguments or seduced by marketing slogans. Everyone feels that, under conditions of careful, transparent and explicit management of change, they have the space to understand where they're being required to go, but which bits are open for negotiation and especially which bits of the path that they use to get there are for them to decide or to negotiate. And then giving them the time and the support to do that . . . it's a big investment . . . but . . . it's a good investment in the long run and really pays off' (Judith George).
- Administrators at higher institutional levels will 'look after their own patch' of institutional territory. Roger Mills learned to accept that fact of competitive institutional dynamics and work with it. Be savvy about contextual politics and power struggles, as David Warr, for example, learned: '. . . all universities are political but this one was Machiavellian. Everybody was scheming against everybody else and my project, I am sure, was being used as a pawn by some people in their own games.'
- Institutional planning 'is not necessarily rational at all. It can be very political' (Greville Rumble). Allied to that argument is the futility of an institution aiming for a 'steady state' existence; not understanding that 'the only certainty is continuous change and that affects everybody'. 'Planners' failures to recognize these points and change-based opportunities may lead to the production of "SPOTS" – "Strategic Plans On The Shelf"' (Greville Rumble).
- Build up your own 'grassroots' experience for reality checks with eager but less than adequately informed colleagues. Do not accept everything you are told by early adopters, technology marketers or even the first researchers into new technologies.
- Maintain the momentum once change processes have begun. If it's lost, 'you have to cycle back a long way' (Lee Taylor).
- Anticipate and avoid mistakes in the early stages of innovation. As Gary Miller, for example, found, 'early mistakes have a very long legacy; [so] you really have to work to overcome [them]'. The innovation idea itself may carry the best intent, the loftiest goals; but that intention will fade against inadequate infrastructure needed for its implementation. Even worse, less than expected results will bring their own set of impacts, as Glen Farrell learned 'in hindsight': 'You're better off not to have tried than to have tried to do something innovative poorly, because it just sets everything back.'

- 'Show success. Explain it. Keep talking, and publicly, even in the face of disinterest or ignorance of the societal implications of distance mode learning' (Bernd Schachstiek). 'You can only survive at the sideline [of conventional university practice] when you are successful. It's easy to kill you there when you're not successful' (Uli Bernath).
- 'Always have a "safety net" ' (John Cowan).

To bridge into the next section, hear this exchange as Tom Prebble drew together his key experiential lessons about how to innovate and manage successful distance modes of teaching within a traditional university:

> *Tom:* [First] find ways for the university people to say 'yes'. Second, don't set yourself up for failure. Third, institutions have a long memory for misfortune. Fourth, persist; reduce the novelty of an innovation. Fifth, make policy by assertion; be assertive about that policy . . . judiciously.
>
> *Liz:* And the last [lesson]: [is it that] most institutional information has low salience [as in most staff do not know what is going on]?
>
> *Tom:* Yes. [pause] I think there's a branding ability too – if you can package your ideas in ways that are understandable and easily communicated.

Institutional administration

Parts of what you have just read could, arguably, be placed in this section. But choices had to be made based on the predominant focus here, and that is infrastructural elements and dynamics. Preparedness and sustainability factors thread through the following experiential lessons about administering the infrastructure needed for quality learning, teaching and guiding students who cannot or prefer not to learn always in walled, time-bound classes on a campus.

Preparedness refers to various areas of practice, especially to needs assessments and staff skill development. What Chère Gibson calls 'forward funding' is crucial – 'you may need two or three or more years of funding in advance of launching any programme'. Terry Gibson learned that when a technology innovation was proposed, the initial financing for purchase 'was the easy part. However there was never enough money to support the necessary human infrastructure and to maintain the technology.'

Another example of the importance of being adequately prepared related to the skill resources of staff. Look past one's own institution to be informed about what colleagues around the world, as well as locally, are doing and writing about. Do this especially when budget constraints apply. Learn whatever business management skills are needed. Be willing to dig into the details, because while grand plans for institutional change may be in effect, they will materialize only if a wise manager begins with the underpinning elements. Changes will be sustainable if managers attend to 'the culture that people have created in which they live and work' (Louise Moran). To attend is to help staff examine ingrained habit and the reassurance of the familiar, and consider the consequences of keeping and abandoning certain routines and goals. As Louise experienced, changes in how staff members see 'professional value' can make some staffers very nervous as they begin the process of owning changed perceptions of self. Finally, attend to the qualities of the current context and design solutions to fit them. Do not rely on old solutions (or think that one can step into the same river twice). Contextual conditions change, and so the change drivers and impacts need clear identification.

Now to infrastructure in general.

An 'effective management system' for course design and delivery is, for John Cowan, essential for today's operations. Related to this emphasis on effectiveness are several participants' observations on the need to integrate the many components of quality-monitored distance mode operations in a conventional university or in an exclusively distance mode one. Despite apparent understanding via listening to a proposal for distance education operations, the action needed to functionally integrate all the pieces will take considerable negotiation and logistics efforts and partnership development. Lee Taylor has learned much about education-focused partnerships: '. . . partnerships aren't based on contractual arrangements; they're based on a common, shared set of values and aims, and then some form of service-level agreement about what each partner is going to contribute towards reaching those common goals'.

Since devolved models of distance mode course provision in universities generally do not work, at least in Claire Matthewson's experience over several decades in various institutions, the most effective infrastructure is an identifiable operation, a system of skills and service criteria for managing consistently the quality of operations with distance mode students and tutors. Devolution of distance mode operations back into various academic departments does not bode well for quality assurance or cost effectiveness. When an identifiable distance mode infrastructure exists (i.e. no devolution), it gains enough power to insist on necessary conditions for good practice. For example: cost-saving in selecting supportable technologies; contracting academics to teach in both conventional (mostly as real time and face-to-face lecturing/discussions) and distance modes; allowing students to use both modes to gain timely courses; and ensuring that once students signed up, they were guaranteed programme completion within a set time period.

The human elements of the infrastructure

There were other experiential lessons in addition to always being intellectually curious, being open to having one's knowledge challenged or enhanced, and being willing to join new professional communities. The goal of being 'a lifelong learner' is important to Gisela Pravda, for example, but she role-modelled the concept: 'Everybody whom I tell that I prepared for and passed the Ph.D. [examinations] after I was pensioned . . . thinks [that] it is impossible that such an old person causes herself so much trouble, mentally speaking.' Uli Bernath emphasized a very broad approach, going 'across cultural borders' to 'understand what the practice looks like, what the quality standards for good practice are, here . . . [because] if you are not open to what's happening around you . . . you will run a very narrow-minded and meagre everyday routine'.

Collaborative styles of working are still key for Janet Poley: 'A lot of consortium leadership is trying to help be clear about directions, making sure that you have support systems. I call it "glue" in a lot of cases . . . it's like [having] to be a crack filler . . . to do the stuff to knit things together to make sure the systems are in place to support the collaborative work.' Sometimes, discreet bribery (as in trading payments with unexpected perquisites) may enhance collaborative activity, especially when the institution wants the very top (but very time-pressed and expensive) experts to assist in developing learning materials. Fred Lockwood's plans for all expenses paid, working weekends away in warm countries for course content experts were very successful for course design creativity, scheduling efficiency and financial savings.

Significant change incurs pain on some people. Other people produce pain for their colleagues when they resist change by presenting arguments based on lack of precedent or reduced autonomy, or strategies such as 'well-poisoning' opposition that negatively affects everyone (Judith Fage). When faced with the kind of 'pain' caused by one's own mistakes, it is best for any staff member to admit them, apologize and offer compensation. Daryl Nation had a lesson about balancing his manager's role of directing staff with the need to create genuine 'volunteerism' toward action; he encouraged staff to give their ideas and explore their reactions to the impending directions. When dealing with teaching staff, another issue – subversion of procedure – needs managing with calm determination: 'you've also got to carefully close off all the options for teaching staff to use their power and influence to subvert the system by getting other people with less power, such as secretaries, to do things'. Alertness to one's position in organizational communications and distance from front-line, day-to-day operations is also necessary, since the front-liners can better anticipate the actual implications of a proposed innovation or change in procedure. Adding to that type of learning, for Judith Fage at least, were two other claims on her alertness as a leader. One refers to the iatrogenic impacts of change, or what she calls 'hostages to fortune': 'changes which were right, but which opened the door for the kind of opportunities that could be damaging'. The other claim refers to the need to act, not adopt an ostrich posture and hide the head: 'Things won't get better by themselves; you've got to do something.'

Financial matters are sites for learning. Know not only where the funding sources exist but also who controls them and how. Gaining grant money for distance teaching operations gains attention in universities, and even some easy academic allies who dream of access to such funds. Tom Prebble learned the lesson of the iceberg's existence: what is seen above the water has to be supported by a massive bulk underneath. So his funding of online learning has been 'an iceberg investment . . . most of [it] has nothing to do with learning; it's been all these infrastructural services, all these single channel strategies so students can do their business with us online'. Not all projects need heavy funding. Louise Moran learned that 'permission and passion and a few pennies' may go a long way in helping staff at all levels learn more skills during funded innovation projects.

Working in the private sector, Bernd Schachstiek learned caution in spending marketing funds: 'Don't believe advertising companies, don't believe people who tell you what is right or wrong; testing, testing and testing is the key to success.'

Personal styles for instigating/managing change

Certain personal characteristics failed to attract value for the participants. Here is the list:

- 'egoists or 'lone rangers' (Michael Lambert);
- carrying 'control freakery' (Lee Taylor);
- having a messiah complex (as in working to save the world);
- being an educational imperialist, holding cultural colonizing tendencies;
- being impatient;
- revealing institutional problems or malicious gossip in public;
- becoming institutionalized (as in remaining too long in one institution);
- looking for intellectual deference from staff;
- posturing over theory-building;
- expecting easy (or any) funding for any good idea;
- assuming one's analyses are always right;
- taking on 'too much responsibility or guilt' for dynamics beyond one's control (Lee Taylor);
- believing in oneself to be a 'fount of all wisdom' (Janet Jenkins).

Many characteristics do attract value:

- being effective team players;
- having a high tolerance for ambiguity;
- being able to 'seize critical moments' (Lee Taylor);
- being willing to admit mistakes;
- trusting more knowledgeable colleagues to 'move things forward' (Lee Taylor);
- being willing to appear eccentric or 'being slightly mad . . . because you are going against the norm . . . bucking tradition' (Louise Moran);
- 'not taking [anything] for granted' in any cultural context (Janet Jenkins);

- being willing to change prized preconceptions about what should be done, and being tactful: '. . . if you want to be a change agent, don't make anybody feel that they are a Luddite' (Glen Farrell).

Patience is key for a group of participants. Hear these examples to see the scope of application. Colin Yerbury learned the value of being willing to walk around his (dual mode) university and talk informally with academics. He regrets that, in today's contexts, 'people don't seem to have the knack of engaging individuals in the academic community in a familial way'. Louise Moran managed patience as an administrative virtue: 'you've got to be willing to go two steps forward and one step back and manage the minutiae as well; and to recognize that you will not achieve real change very fast; which conflicts with demands that you make changes fast'. When once watching a lengthy policy negotiation, Roger Mills learned the value of waiting: '[Keep] your [gun] powder dry' – use restraint and political astuteness to delay suggesting a preferred solution until everyone else has reached desperation stage and the deadline is imminent. Shona Butterfield reflected on gaining patience for decision-making:

> I did learn that it was important for me to wait because when I reacted and made the decision, invariably if I made it too early, I regretted it. So people knew that when I was clear about something, I was very quick to decide. And when I wasn't, I got better about explaining what was happening for me so that they knew what was going on.

Over his long career, day by day, project by project, John Thomas internalized the patience to accumulate his skill repertoire.

Possessing the humility to listen respectfully to all stakeholders, local opinion, the critics of any proposed innovation and to one's staff, is an asset, not a weakness. No confrontations, blunt talk or delusions of superiority. Instead, '[find] the level of comfort a society needs to accept a new idea . . . listen, listen and listen . . . [do] not try and impose your way as the only clever and sensible way to overcome challenges or . . . problems' (Raj Dhanarajan). Brian Kenworthy quickly learned that any pre-planned strategies for helping colleagues in other countries would likely hold little value for the new context, so his reliance on 'local knowledge and local expertise' was crucial. Tactful suggestions given from a collegial rather than a command position will likely lead to greater cooperation. David Warr explains: '. . . you don't say, "Right, we will do this to learn it that way". You say, "Well, I heard in another country they tried this; shall we do it? Shall we try it together?" ' Avoiding educational imperialism was also important for Tony Dodds: 'We were not just transporting British experience to developing countries.' As Janet Jenkins learned to be quite 'willing to adapt to unexpected circumstances', Greville Rumble learned to be 'prepared to dump the procedures . . . and adapt [the] frameworks quite quickly'. Having some humility about one's own skill limits and acknowledging some higher levels of staff expertise helps, and especially during times of significant change: 'Any paradigm shift eventually comprehends every aspect of the universe. One person simply cannot master all of that' (Dan Granger).

Finale

It is appropriate to conclude with one participant who reached out directly and personally to you, the reader.

> [You need] to maintain your own sense of self and your own sense of expertise in order to provide a keel to your own work. Otherwise you're going to be buffeted by the different winds and currents involved in change – pushing you about technology, pushing you about teaching and learning, pushing you about administration, pushing you about enrolment, etc. You need to know what your centre is, and how to maintain that.
>
> (Dan Granger)

6

Looking forward

Liz Burge

Looking towards the future needs various activities: recognizing changed contexts; naming trends or issues of concern; deciding which experiential lessons might be offered as advice for less experienced colleagues; and considering what new knowledge might be constructed in research to sustain future practice. This chapter summarizes the informed opinions of experts who have already looked forward.

The chapter ends with a synthesis of all the reflections from the participants.

Responses relevant for this chapter were usually quite pithy, i.e. meaningful but concise. A few participants did not offer comments specific enough to be included here, especially if they had given related reflections earlier.

Recognizing changed contexts

Most opinions centred on learners and learning, the impacts of technology, institutional change and public recognition.

Learners and learning

Compared to learners of 20 years ago, today's learners are more sophisticated, especially in terms of their own technology skills, and have significantly reduced attitudes of deference or gratitude toward educational personnel. Carrying a client attitude, they demand efficient services, especially because of their time-pressed lifestyles, stress-related jobs, and the speed and information capacity of online environments. They are now 'very pragmatic': 'looking for the quality of experience to suit them at a price they can afford with outcomes that are accredited' (Lee Taylor). While one participant sees older students, others see increased numbers of younger ones, using distance modes to help them move faster through their studies in more traditional campus settings. In the UK, the impact of equal opportunities regulations in higher education caused a 'seismic shift' in women's enrolments, with subsequent impacts on distance mode provision (Lee Taylor). While most career training will remain institution-based (formal), non-formalized and self-directed learning for adults via electronic databases and online communications will 'revolutionize' how adults think about learning (Ros Morpeth).

Several participants acknowledged that the learner-centred approaches so often discussed in postsecondary education since the late twentieth century are now 'regarded as appropriate, justifiable and something to be encouraged' (Daryl Nation), especially regarding the acquisition of learning-to-learn skills. But one contrary view came from John Cowan: his experience leads him to think that students 'are not being helped to learn' because they are getting 'less and less support. And so there's less and less learning happening. And less and less deep learning happening.'

Where distance mode courses have been designed to high quality and flexibility standards, a ripple effect has expanded their use into contiguous (face-to-face) classrooms. The major international example of team-based quality assurance of course materials – the Open University (UK) (OUUK):

> set new standards for pedagogy and ... also took distance education into a whole new area in terms of developing instructional design ... [the result was] learning materials that even at their worst are very good, and at their best are absolutely superb ... it got distance education taken seriously as a method of doing higher education.
>
> (John Thomas)

Raj Dhanarajan notes a significant development: 'We have found tools to match the talents of our learners. We are beginning to use tools to enable our learners to learn for themselves.' Reusable learning objects (RLOs) – as indicators of change in teaching – attracted very few comments. Gary Miller believes, however, that progress is evident:

> *Gary:* ... we will break apart the courses and sell the individual modules and then everybody will assemble the modules around their own sense of the curriculum.
> *Liz:* Like a sort of cognitive Lego system?
> *Gary:* Exactly, yes.

Impacts of technology

These drew many comments, most relating to dramatic changes in ease and speed of communications for learning and for greater institutional system efficiencies. Today's technologies are 'so much simpler ... so much more reliable ... and much more transparent [to use]' (Donald McDonell).

Much reputable 'grey' (not commercially published) literature for credit courses and for the distance education field itself is now on the internet (via organizational websites), thus increasing access and distribution opportunities. Software for institutional operations has streamlined and enhanced methods of quality assurance. Educators gain greater choice in decision-making because more delivery options exist. E-learning software and learners' individual access to internet-based information of varying levels of complexity have produced significant (if yet inadequately assessed) changes: '[it] gives the person more importance, it individualizes learning in a way that we have never known about' (Gisela Pravda). Increasingly, faculty members in conventional universities are adopting higher-end technologies for teaching, but are bypassing lower-end, often less expensive, and still effective communication technologies. Thus, reduced, or even denial of, access becomes an issue for adults who cannot afford the purchase and/or usage costs of the higher-end technology.

Institutional change

Blurring the boundaries between contiguous and distance modes of learning and teaching, i.e. creating more flexible or blended forms of programming for students, and naming it as such, is leading to greater public acceptance of these modes of provision and a departure from naming educators by the formats they use: 'not distance educators, not "traditional campus" educators, but educators open to all sorts of possibilities' (Greville Rumble). Today's demands for institutional generation of revenue and today's commercialization of higher education, i.e. playing to the most lucrative market segments and to economic productivity needs, rather than taking a more liberal approach and producing 'cultured, educated, well-rounded human beings' (Greville Rumble), drew some comments of regret and concern.

While globalized institutional operations are seen by many participants as a major change, several recognize the difficulties of sending course materials, technology and policy from one culture and national economy to another. Greville Rumble's words were echoed by others: 'distance education clearly can be globalized because the technology enables it [but] there are particular issues surrounding globalization – some of which are ethical, some of which are cultural – which we haven't explored'.

The OUUK itself did not escape notice. Several participants saw how its institutional evaluation strategies have undergone change from externally run, rather inspectorial operations to self-directed, reflective, internal data gathering and analysis against self-expressed mission goals. Its sheer size, limits of curricula offerings relative to some conventional universities, and competition from smaller, fast-moving universities keen to capture more market share, have produced new strategies for growth – making judicious partnerships with otherwise potential competitors, attending to new professional development needs in organizations and sophisticated niche marketing. Broadening the institutional view, Ros Morpeth sees both areas of post-secondary activity changing:

> As technology has moved on so much, those institutions that were dedicated to distance education are having to cope with much greater change than the traditional universities have had to cope with. And distance education itself has become part of the portfolio of most of the traditional institutions. So in those fundamental ways the whole context has changed.

Public recognition

Two opinions best represent what are seen as positive changes in reputation. Michael Lambert sees the biggest change in distance education as being its 'overall acceptance . . . because of what happened in the nineties in terms of technology and all the prestigious universities going into online learning. We naturally benefited from that.' Ros Morpeth is equally pragmatic: 'distance education is no longer sort of seen as the last resort or the low cost option. It's actually seen as a way of opening up access, or, if you're the University of Phoenix, expanding your markets dramatically.'

Consider this broad view of perceived change before we move on:

> Between 1971 and 2005 the fundamentals [of distance education] have remained the same. It is all about access . . . about increasing participation and about taking learning to where your clients . . . or learners are . . . But the changes that have occurred are in the effectiveness and efficiencies in the way we have dealt with the issues. The changes have been about the tools that we have used and the environmental [conditions] around the fundamentals; [they] are all the time changing. Some of [those conditions are] for the better; and others, I'm not so sure . . . There has to be a case made for education for education's sake in order to have a very healthy and vibrant society that cares, that contributes, that practises democracy, that presents ideas and challenges, and chases after big ideals.
>
> (Raj Dhanarajan)

Naming concerns

Generally, the topics attracting most concern were access, knowledge about the field (covered above), learning design issues, commodification and marketization, technology applications and policy development.

Access

As are some other participants, Chère Gibson is concerned about the denial of access for some potential students as institutions move to 'higher and higher technology solutions . . . [based on the] "mono-medium" of online technology'. She believes also that too many operations today show signs of 'being driven more by dollars than by equity' as institutions seek the more lucrative programme markets. Reluctance by governments to invest the funds necessary to create more affordable education and 'equity of access' is creating a secondary problem. Terry Gibson echoed some other participants: 'those who can afford it, get it; and those who can't, even their choices are diminished'. In terms of specific populations needing better access, references were made to learners with disabilities and the large numbers of teachers and other workers (e.g. farmers) in developing countries struggling to become better formally qualified. Effective access implies flexibility in programming according to the needs of adults at varying levels of educational preparation and need; Tony Dodds wonders why universities could not give 'credibility and status' to more flexible attitudes and procedures that met learners on the learners' terms.

Learning design issues

Concerns here related mostly to learner characteristics and choice, skill sets, course quality and student support. Regarding demographics in conventional institutions, 'the main need is . . . not [to] think of the students as 18- to 21-year-old elite, white, males' (Tony Bates). The provision of adequate choice in media and learning designs is not a given for some participants. Helping 'regular' academics to reduce or stop lecturing via distance modes and learn new skills for 'teaching students differently and better [is] . . . the hardest challenge' (Tony Bates). In her concern with the related issue of being a 'learning coach', Shona Butterfield argued that:

> Institutions aren't adequately yet facing up to clearly identifying what kinds of students they are there to serve, and then matching the kind of delivery to that. That may well mean that they want a mix of modes, but they're not yet at the way of thinking, 'within one course we might need a couple of options here'.

The drive for high quality learning materials (not just any popular textbook plus a rapidly produced study guide) and consistently high standards of academic learning support and outcomes cannot be taken for granted. Hilary Perraton sees a lot of questions about the model of distance learning that will work with not very educationally sophisticated young learners: 'In the studies for example at some of the Asian universities I think you will find we are getting pretty poor results in terms of graduation rates and that bothers me because of the expectations and the disappointments for the people that have been signed up.'

Examining web-based courses has led Fred Lockwood into some disappointments because he sees too much 'poor quality'; for example, poorly developed objectives and layout, cognitively weak in-text questions for the learner, and little guidance for critical reading. His conclusion about such material: 'It's a caricature . . . and that's what I really worry about; it's a result of pushing the [marketing] idea that "We're becoming a flexible learning university; we have embodied the best features of both distance and flexible learning".'

When conventional universities adopt distance mode programming, might their cultural traditions of fixed schedules for on-campus operations reduce the flexibility of 'true' distance education? Dominique Abrioux thinks so, and he is concerned: '. . . both the content and the delivery methods become less flexible. How do you match that with the need for lifelong learning? Because lifelong learning means flexibility: you have to be allowed to do it around other activities.'

He is also not persuaded that distance and online learning is as available an answer to students' learning problems as it ought to be. The adequate provision of student support is of concern to many participants, with comments focused mainly on issues of its priority when it is perceived as a comparatively costly service in institutions looking for ultra cost-efficient operations. Some universities are using basic distance education modes to enrol large numbers of students (and thus generate revenue) but then deny the students adequate support or quality in course designs because, they argue, costs must be contained.

Commodification and marketization concerns nest in business language adopted by many universities, curricula choice, funding and 'cultural imperialism' arising from globalization goals (Ronnie Carr). Many comments were heard about a problem that Louise Moran explained as the 'arid concept' of 'education as an industry' and university activity as preoccupied with 'utilitarian vocational preparation' instead of valuing higher education as a value in itself, assisting the production of 'a civil society'. When online packages are sold and created as attractively cheap commodities from efficient 'production lines' without much attention to where the professor or tutor fits in, then Donald McDonell and Janet Poley would become concerned. How financing is secured and played out by fund-chasing private institutions becomes a concern for Janet:

> Basically a lot of these [online colleges] went to see where the government was going to give subsidies, and then developed online programmes [then went] to the public universities to get the faculty out of [them] on contract, and then charged three times as much tuition as the public universities. So that means you can only educate one-third as many people . . . And then they call it profit. I don't like that.

Technology applications

Essentially, those who commented here focused on hardware and software types of technology. They are concerned about over-reliance on a single technology 'as panacea' (Raj Dhanarajan), technology-driven thinking, the seductive power of technology hyperbole and how it is linked to expectations of revenue, and the 'divide' between the technology-rich and the technology-poor. Since the chapter on technology illuminates these areas, just one reflection may suffice here: '... television and video ... didn't transform education, but just became one of a number of components in distance programmes ... we need to get things into perspective' (Ronnie Carr).

Policy development

Various concerns were mentioned; all complex and needing more time than was available. Some had been mentioned earlier while focused on other topics. Designing flexible government funding mechanisms to account for how and when adults want to learn over their lifespan and confronting the financial limits of stabilized tuition fees within the rising costs of postsecondary institutions drew attention. 'Many institutions haven't got a clue in terms of what it's really costing them to finance their distance education programme; that there are just so many costs buried in this lump called "overhead" ' (Terry Gibson).

Ensuring that laws about the quality of education cover more than just consumer-oriented, legal aspects, developing government policy that acknowledges the processes and goals of distance modes, and constructing national government budgeting for lifespan learning appeared as possible solutions to some concerns. When an institution reaches 'middle age' and shows more operational formality and hierarchy, with reduced informal access to leadership, and output measures that do not match earlier social justice-related goals: such changes were sources of regret for one participant.

One final concern tugs at realities rarely revealed. But such realities might be analysed and reported with the same kinds of courage, enquiry, determination and passion for excellence shown in earlier chapters:

> The trouble is [that] ... in the real world, costs blow out, technologies fail to deliver, teaching remains untransformed, students don't learn or don't complete the course, managements and systems falter, territorial disputes arise and faculty receive inadequate training, time release and support for their work. Yet these matters are rarely reported on in the research of ICT or open and distance learning. (Colin Latchem)

Offering advice

A relatively small number of participants decided that any advice from them would have much less impact than if less experienced colleagues reflected on their own experience, in order to 'find their own way' (David Warr). Most participants did have some specific advice, categorized into being self-aware and self-respecting, having humility and grace, being knowledgeable, constructing knowledge, and doing creative and critical thinking.

Being self-aware and self-respecting

- 'Avoid too much self doubt – especially women!' (Judith Fage).
- 'Don't give up! Stick to your conviction!' (Gisela Pravda).
- 'Focus. Learn to say no. Get good survival tactics . . . take yourself seriously' (Judith George).
- 'Don't get pigeonholed just because you're a generalist. Know what you can do and recognize that other people can be more expert at certain things. If you are broadly a generalist you can still make your contributions' (Lee Taylor).
- '. . . listen to what your experience and your heart are telling you. If it seems wrong, it probably is wrong; and weigh up the consequences of speaking out about that and where you choose to speak out . . . Be a plain speaker. Understand the political context . . . make sure that you trust and respect the people who are managing and leading the organization in which you're working' (Lee Taylor).
- 'It's about being professional in a profession . . . it's something about self-accountability as well as enforced accountability. And the day you lose that, you're just a human resource' (Maggie Coats).

Having humility and grace

What I call humility represents an attitude of mind and knowledge about how innovations are best adopted, as well as respectful listening and thinking strategies that acknowledge the limits of one's skills. Some key examples follow:

- 'Don't expect to go online, be an immediate success, and know exactly what you're going to be doing' (Brian Kenworthy).
- 'Listen; pay attention to people who don't necessarily see the world as you see it and learn from it' (Janet Poley).

Other leaders agree. 'Listen to the people. Listen to your students. It's the best source for knowing what you should do, even better than asking experts. Sorry for that [laughs]' (Bernd Schachtsiek). Michael Lambert's metaphor, 'Don't get too far in front of your own parade', or Brian Kenworthy's advice for teamwork that avoids the 'up-front stars' problem, carried the same intent as Raj Dhanarajan's advice:

> [Don't] run away with that arrogance of being far ahead of your time; but ask 'What is the purpose of me being ahead of my time? The purpose is to ensure that my community is going to derive a lot of benefits from my foresight.' Then you owe it to yourself, especially, to slow down and address the concerns of the people from whom you find yourself being ahead.

To academics, Roger Mills offers this advice: 'acknowledge that there are . . . instructional designers who can help you get across your knowledge better than you can. Because that is their profession. You're an academic. Your job . . . is to generate knowledge and help students to learn.' Donald McDonell did that – with his professorial peers. He enabled them to learn from each other about their teaching innovations; it was not for him, even as the expert in technology applications, to adopt a transmissive model of teaching and simply tell them what to think.

Being gracious (my term) was advised. How would one distinguish this quality from everyday good manners? Find the time to support others, be tolerant of others' mistakes, learn from them, and move on. Acknowledge (publicly) good work in others, and mentor colleagues through difficult periods.

Being knowledgeable

This advice referred to the published work of predecessors and colleagues' activities in current contexts. Most participants felt strongly about being knowledgeable.

Three strategies were embedded in advice to know the literature:

- Avoid thinking that nothing older than five years is worth reading, for that betrays a lack of respect and an ignorance of the transferability of knowledge and of long-term innovation cycles.
- Read the literature before jumping into action, to avoid 'reinventing the wheel', suffering the 'bandwagon effect' (uncritical copying of fashion) or experiencing loss of respect from wiser colleagues.
- Avoid dismissing the work of earlier generations as irrelevant, because 'there is some accumulated wisdom and experience in the field that is worth getting at' (Greville Rumble). As Claire Matthewson argued, 'The new generation of distance or flexible educators doesn't know or [thinks it needs] to know about the theory and praxis foundations of what they're doing . . . If you don't know what the fight was and what it was about, you don't know what it is you have to protect.'

Inside one's institution, know the complex contextual dynamics, political and financial as well as educational, especially considering that just 'being right doesn't win the day' (Dan Granger). Know enough about the levers of power to inform only those who really need to know about a proposed or under-trial innovation. For better problem-solving and innovation, 'look outside [one's own institution] . . . take the blinkers off' (Fred Lockwood). As Tom Prebble argued:

> there is no right answer, but there are better answers in certain contexts and . . . if . . . you've had a chance to reflect on a range of different milieux, you've got a fair chance of coming up with an appropriate answer for your situation; as opposed to just buying the first solution that you come across.

Staying current, however, takes daily effort, as Michael Lambert learnt: 'You cannot sit at a desk and expect to have the world report to you every day . . . you have to work at it! . . . there is no substitute for reading voraciously and scanning the educational environment for changes'.

Being a creative and critical thinker

Such thinking styles (as distinct from thinking about critical incidents) apply particularly to technology applications. There is no single solution. Know the context of use before selecting a technology mix. Be compulsive about the details that underpin operational success. Echoing Hilary Perraton's advice to be sceptical at all times, Gail Crawford advised 'quit looking for panaceas . . . it is the media assumption that when we have a new tool [it's a case of thinking] "now I've got my hammer, every problem begins to look like a nail" '. Recognize that sustainable and effective change takes time for its implementation. Make no assumptions about 'technological leap-frogging', i.e. assuming that a developing country can 'jump over' older technologies and adopt new ones:

> In Malawi they . . . have had to increase the size of the print font on their printed material because so many more people these days are studying by candlelight again . . . learning about the context, really, is the key to it . . . I'd be suspicious of anybody who assumes that online learning is accessible to anybody who wants to learn something. We have to look critically at that.
>
> (Patrick Guiton)

Tony Dodds reinforced this principle of context-relevance: '[use] the technology from the field end, rather than from the administrative and technological end'. Finally, learn to reconcile two opposing tasks: being creative and informed enough to develop a substantial vision, but also being attentive to the smaller, but make-or-break, operational details without them being distractive (Janet Poley). Thinking outside the conventional framing of problems and solutions (or 'the box') is important for Janet.

Consider some implications nesting inside these two offers of advice:

Passion will take you a long way . . . [and] through the rough times. We need to continue to remember why we are doing this, who it is we are trying to work with – those learners who for whatever reason need access to education and training, be it credit or non-credit. We just need to keep learners and learning to the fore: they really are central to the enterprise. We need to be reflective. And . . . we need to get beyond simply launching programmes. After 150 years we are still running around so busy doing, we are not writing enough about what we are doing and we are not doing enough action research on what we are doing to really grow a scholarly field to the extent that I think it should be grown.

(Chère Gibson)

If you're a young person in higher education now wanting to improve access, then the 'think big, act small' principle applies; the 'choose your technologies wisely and to the maximum variety you can afford' applies; the 'learn how to use those technologies before you actually embark on them' applies; the 'encourage your organization . . . to develop systems and processes that will support you in making those courses accessible' applies; 'teaching your management, forcibly if necessary, that they have to change their traditional ways of thinking' applies. [Teach] yourself and your management and your colleagues that what you're talking about is part of the mainstream; flexibility in teaching and learning is not marginal any more.

(Louise Moran)

Constructing knowledge

Learning processes

Learning processes and administrative/infrastructure matters captured most attention here, with other suggestions focusing on technology applications, teaching, evaluation, access and change/innovation. No order of priority governs the listing.

- Roles and results of contiguous contexts (e.g. residencies), as integrated with non-contiguous contexts of learning (e.g., online) (Chère Gibson).
- Evidence-based research into 'what makes a difference to learner outcomes' that avoids 'unreplicated, small sample stuff' (Shona Butterfield).
- Effectiveness of the constructivist model of learning.
- Actual impact of feedback on assignments to students; would a feed-forward approach work better?
- Ongoing and often work-related learning needs of adults whose jobs depend on accurate knowledge and skill sets but whose training or education should be context-relevant and not necessarily be sourced from institutions far away.

- Multi-tasking inside learning, regardless of technologies in use for the course: 'how well do students learn when they are multi-tasking and what kind of learning do they have? Do they learn more at a superficial level or do they miss things or do they do just as well multi-tasking or not?' (Tony Bates).
- Compare 'the process of conventional education and virtual education' (Hilary Perraton). Rather than limiting the scope to gathering data on the 'type or quality of email interaction between tutor and student', look for more complex and nuanced details about the 'conceptually difficult' territory in holistic approaches.
- Learning process relationships between on-screen and off-screen learning activity, and any consequent changes in power relationships between learner and academic expert/tutor.
- How adults may 'really create intellectual and civic and moral value around information' in technology-mediated environments (Gary Miller).

Administrative/infrastructure

New research into administrative and infrastructure issues would cover policy development, financial issues, transfer of credit and information-sharing:

- 'What kinds of policies . . . in relation to open, flexible learning and what supports and what hinders the development' (Shona Butterfield).
- 'How [the development of China and India] may affect this whole inter-change of education . . . which at the moment is being seen as part of trade and services? Is there ever going to be a global open university?' (David Hawkridge).
- National-level policies concerning distance modes of provision for post-secondary education, for 'clarifying options and educating policy-makers rather than discovering entirely new knowledge or just uncovering existing knowledge' (Tom Prebble).
- A system for 'transparency of credit acceptance' in the USA, regardless of the original source of accreditation (Michael Lambert).
- Using action research, developing locally-owned models for systemic and institutional educational innovation and change, especially for quality assurance and access.
- The actual, not assumed, financial needs for part-time learners: '. . . as tuition becomes more of a barrier, is it a barrier equally for part-time learners?' (Dominique Abrioux).
- 'Price-sensitivity' – where tuition fees meet student limits; or, in Dominique Abrioux's question, 'what is the value of flexibility to the individual and to society? . . . I think it is going to become increasingly important.'
- Business models for online, private educational institutions, and for all forms of open and flexible distance learning.
- 'Why is it that something that's so appealing from a common-sense point

of view, given all of our declarations around the world about increased access to especially higher learning, that our institutions of higher learning have continued to marginalize the value or the usefulness of distance learning? . . . And yet the noise around technology, using technology to take learning across to deprived communities, it's very very high. It's a social-political question to chase after . . . is there another agenda that [we're] not able to crack open and see inside?' (Raj Dhanarajan).

Technology applications

- 'We still haven't worked out cheap ways to educate students to be able to work in hypertext' as authors or programmers (Daryl Nation).
- Integrative and innovative uses of all possible technologies – old and new, hard-wired and 'human-wired', software and 'warmware', audio and visual/text forms – for real value in learning, and for diverse contexts, e.g. using laptops and satellites with nomadic peoples.
- Buildings as technology designs – research and test designs for 'performance space in academic communities . . . [gain a] balance of creative team space and individual space' (Lee Taylor).

Teaching

- Look at effectiveness ratios of virtual to actual practice in performance skill learning.
- Since the best associate lecturers (tutors) in the OUUK tend to be 'self-exploiting' (Maggie Coats), how might that attitude be better rewarded and built upon for professional growth?
- 'Why open and distance learning has not been more widely used [and on larger scales] for adult basic and non-formal education' (Tony Dodds).

Evaluation (especially formative methods)

- Quality assurance for different models of delivery in various environments.
- 'The effectiveness of different interventions . . . can you have a nurse in a quiet time taking a five-minute chunk of learning; does that make any difference?' (Lee Taylor).
- How, definitively, to improve course and programme completion rates. Should the 'problem' of course 'drop outs' be re-framed to show more respect for learners' judgments and adaptive decision-making?
- Gather 'more output data because we are very short on it; [especially in] developing countries' (Hilary Perraton). Also important for him are finding correlations between outcomes and the best quality course designs and tutoring support.

- Assess outcomes in terms of 'return on investment, including total cost of ownership, revenues and cost savings where appropriate; student achievement, including comparisons with other learning modalities; scalability, including technical infrastructure and support resources; and collaboration on content functionality and best practices' (Shona Butterfield, reading from a report and arguing that all four are 'fundamental' topics for research).
- 'Open source models for providing infrastructure for supporting learning for the future' (Shona Butterfield).

Access

The most often mentioned orientation was to question whether current distance provision (including online formats) has actually increased access to needy groups or is even preparing to cope with the diverse educational demands of the world's expanding population. Dan Granger's guess is that '[access] would be not as great as everybody assumes', especially for workplace education. Access may be reduced and learning outcomes affected when educators change the mediating technology, ignore the financial limits of adults to pay fees, or fail to provide adequate access to quality information sources. So questions regarding those possible impacts need researching. Where 'widening participation' programmes are in place, more effectiveness evaluation is needed.

Change/innovation

In general, the few suggestions here focused on more studies that use replicative and/or longitudinal approaches to change; and, using long-term views of innovation and change cycles, conducting more sector-focused and professionally researched histories of distance education.

Part 3

The commentators meta-reflect

7

From *Educating Rita* to iPods and beyond

Michael Collins

Introduction

The reflections on practice are highly relevant, I believe, for all postsecondary educators who know what the advancement of adult learning principles in their institutions entails. They confirm, with authority and heart, that the salient issues, pedagogical commitments and strategies, and ongoing aspirations concerning the development of distance education for adults have been well understood and have found wide support among adult educators like myself. My observations on how these aspirations play out are guided, in part, by Paulo Freire's (1981) dialogic problem-posing pedagogy; recognized in adult education as an antidote to what Freire describes as the 'banking concept' of education – the mere dissemination of information to students for regurgitation on request from the teacher. I agree with the interviewees about avoiding educational practices that serve to impose a 'banking concept' approach. However, from a critical perspective and based on long experience as an adult educator, I am concerned with the over-emphasis placed on the application of technique and the deployment of technology in education. Elsewhere, I have argued (Collins 1991, 1998), along with other educational critics, that this tendency operates to distort conventional views on curriculum design, teaching practice and the learning processes. Using a critical perspective as well, I discern how pedagogical practices (including distance education) have been re-shaped according to market model criteria and increasingly imposed on public education institutions during the past two decades.

'Flexible higher education', argue the interviewees, should mean easier access for adult learners, providing more options to accommodate varying learner needs and alternative modes of course design and programme development. Not so well observed in the findings is the managerial concept of 'flexible higher education' that, in line with a business corporate model, is increasingly evident on university campuses worldwide (Collins 1998; Woodhouse, 2001). This flexibility trend legitimizes the restructuring of institutional decision-making processes to accelerate management innovations for transforming the campus culture. Management agendas are driven, in part, by the marketization of the universities and are accompanied by an emphasis on entrepreneurship (Currie and Newson 1998; Clark 2001). But those agendas bring growing fears about the loss of academic freedom. For better or worse, distance education is inevitably caught up (complicit, some critics would argue) with this managerial approach to 'flexible higher education' through which students are positioned as consumer units. I recall some of the significant early contributions made by the Open University (UK) to distance education, and then introduce two important concepts – system' and 'lifeworld' – that have implications for the section on technology.

Observations on the Open University (UK)

We are left in no doubt of the Open University's unrivalled position as flagship of distance education open learning systems in higher education; for example, in John Thomas's words: '[it] set new standards for pedagogy and they also took distance education into a whole new area in terms of developing instructional design . . . it got distance education taken seriously as a method of doing higher education'.

Over 35 years after its establishment, the Open University was rated, in 2005 and 2006, the top university in England and Wales for 'student satisfaction' – a huge endorsement in this era of university league tables and the enthronement of marketplace criteria in higher education. Marketplace ideology aside, the sterling reputation now enjoyed by the Open University is a tribute to the moral commitment and political determination of Jennie Lee (Arts Minister in Harold Wilson's Labour government of 1964) who played a key role in the founding of the Open University, and to Walter Perry, the institution's first vice-chancellor, who was largely responsible for deciding that the Open University was not to compromise on academic standards.

For Jennie Lee, a democratic socialist, the Open University was to be part of a larger quest towards social equality in the UK that would, more immediately, allow working-class men and women to reap the benefits of a university education which, hitherto, had been beyond their reach. Walter Perry (1976) was prominent among those who insisted from the outset, and in the face of widespread scepticism, that the new institution would compare favourably with established universities, and especially that Open University courses and degrees would be of equal value to non-distance mode universities. Few would argue with an assessment that Perry's intentions have been more completely realized than those of Jennie Lee.

The blockbuster 1983 movie, *Educating Rita*, about a 26-year-old hairdresser just enrolled at the Open University, was viewed initially by some Open University advocates as tending too much towards caricature. Yet *Educating Rita* touched on issues and concerns that I believe remain relevant for any discussion of the meaning of distance education for mature students in a university setting. Among the increasing number of women 'going back to school' as mature students, some can confirm that the kind of opposition that Rita faced from family and friends may be less overt but still occurring; as are feelings of guilt and isolation, of being torn between the responsibilities carried in their paid work, unpaid house management work and study (von Prümmer 2000). Despite contextual conflicts, Rita prevailed. I am not surprised, based on what we know of adults' intrinsic motivation to persist, sometimes against major institutional and interpersonal challenges. Yet through the character of Rita's initially reluctant Open University tutor, the disillusioned poet and alcoholic Dr Frank Bryant, the movie invites us to question the unquestioned assumption that the acquisition of a university education will create enlightenment in the lives of practical, spontaneous and already intellectually alert people like Rita. Frank even suggests that the academic experience Rita craves serves only to stifle her remarkable spontaneity and creative learning capacities.

As a full-time faculty member at a local traditional university, Frank is an embarrassment to his colleagues. Despite the heavy cynicism and mounting problems with drink that fuel his biting remarks, we may discern a measure of truth in Frank's assessments of the shortcomings of academic life. Rita, initially awe-struck by the world of academics and university students, is at first puzzled and then angered by what she sees as Frank's supercilious contempt for academic work and fellow academics. Ultimately, she reasons that there is some real justification for his jaundiced view of the academy, but her response is more measured: becoming an exemplary mature student, she learns from the academy and her intellectually challenging Open University tutor, happily celebrating her academic success. Frank (quite properly) learns from his student and finds some redemption before leaving for a new life overseas.

Without idealizing the role of the Open University or making icons of Jennie Lee and Walter Perry, and as a counter to the crass commercialization of today's publicly-funded universities which casts the academic as entrepreneur, it is useful to keep in mind today Lee's and Perry's aspirations for open access to academic learning.

System and lifeworld

Drawing substantially from the work of Collins (1991), Mezirow (1995) and Welton (1993, 1995), Jennifer Sumner (2000) argued that distance education serves system rather than lifeworld interests. 'System' refers to bureaucratic and economic (i.e. 'coded by money') imperatives that are legitimated, advanced and imposed in a predominantly non-dialogic authoritarian way from the standpoint of technical (instrumental) rationality. Technical rationality prevails where questions of *means* (a preoccupation with techniques, strategies, tactics and system imperatives) take over *ends* (a concern for what ought to be done). The lifeworld, simply expressed, refers us to the practical projects, feelings and attitudes that make up our everyday life. It is the source of central values and of commitments that emerge in community. The life-world, then, is where our sense of belonging and security is derived. In this vein, aligning distance educators with 'anti-communicative' system impera-tives, Sumner thus responds to my claim (which she cites) that 'more critical analysis is needed to assess the homogenizing effects of distance education and its potential as a delivery system to serve government and large scale corporate interests rather than those of people in their community settings' (Collins 1991: 99).

Four well-informed commentators confirmed the relevance of Sumner's critique. Atthill (2001), for example, argued that any attempt to encourage critical analysis and reflection is 'therefore welcome' (p. 85). Then, echoing other respondents, she wondered whether the critical questions Sumner poses are entirely fair (p. 86), given that colleagues in similar institutional and community-based settings are equally and just as inevitably engaged in serving system imperatives while at the same time expressing genuine moral commitment to the lifeworld interests that these system imperatives under-mine. Such contradictions, I argue, are inherent to conditions under late corporate and state capitalism. If we have to work with these contradictions, it is better we understand more clearly how they affect our action in terms of their constraints and opportunities.

The interviewees understand the need to defend and sustain lifeworld interests, especially as these relate to the life experience of adult learners. Much emphasis is placed on a conviction that technology deployment is not a primary concern for distance education and should not be allowed to steer the learning processes. At the same time, however, the findings are charac-terized by a seemingly non-problematic emphasis concerning the use of technology, with little discernment of the contradictions entailed or of the way technology deployment can shape psychological and social learning processes.

In reply to her respondents, Sumner acknowledged that they contributed significantly to the 'on-going discussion [that] I feel must take place as the practice of distance education meets the juggernaut of corporate globaliza-tion' (pp. 94–5). Critical to opening up the debate, I believe, are Atthill's questions: 'Why are we doing this, whose interests are served by what we are doing, should we be doing something different? Are we doing the right thing?' (2001: 87). These questions have been partially identified for us by the interviewees. Yet Atthill and Sumner are right: these questions must remain open for more thorough critical analysis and debate. Here is an example of how I would begin such an analysis regarding technology use.

On technology innovation

There is considerable consensus among the interviewees that a focus on technology innovation should not take precedence over practical concerns for creating educational experiences in line with the needs of adult learners. Claire Matthewson is clear: 'There are many distances out there . . . technology is not the ultimate answer'. Terry Gibson asserts that 'the technology of the moment is secondary'. Yet it is the discourse on technology adoption and deployment that, to a very large extent, sets out distance education as a distinctive field of professional practice with its designated distance education specialists and instructional designers. The 'early adopters' (Rogers 2003) (especially the most adept 'tekkies' among them) play an important role here, even though the general view of the interviewees' advice is to create boundaries around the seeming significance of early adopters' claims, using managed stages of technology adoption as a key strategy. In this discussion on the ramifications of adoption and deployment, Judith George exclaimed, 'we needed a pedagogy for this technology'. It is difficult, however, to see how such a pedagogy can distance itself from system imperatives (the management of technology adoption) and a technical rationality from which they derive legitimacy.

To suggest that 'new technologies' are 'value neutral' is misleading. *The medium is the message* (McLuhan 1967), indicating that the new technologies have agency in ways that simply cannot be corralled by educators. From the adoption of the weaving loom (the Luddite resistance to this enforced technology innovation was not so irrational as some would imply) to the iPod and beyond, new technologies radically alter cognitive styles (including how people as communities learn and collaborate). They re-shape how we experience the world. A well-researched study on the spread of mobile communication (Katz and Aakhus 2002) confirms this claim about a development that is readily discernible, especially in the lives of younger people. In this view, new technology innovation has a momentum of its own, permeating all aspects of everyday life. So there is less necessity for educators to be concerned about falling behind in not immediately joining a cutting edge quest to adopt new communications technology. Apart from the influence of the 'early adopters', incoming students and educators will bring the technology that is already shaping their everyday lives.

So my advice for educators who view the practical aims of distance education as a vocational commitment is not to sweat it. The early adopters are part of a typical innovation process (Rogers 2003) whereby the latest innovation (e.g. a technology) reaches the attention of key decision-makers. Yet we are well advised to be sceptical of the misplaced enthusiasms of early adopters, especially with regard to costly e-learning initiatives. A notable example is the UK New Labour government's aborted nationwide e-learning endeavour, which allocated £62 million from the public purse for a project to be run by private sector interests (MacLeod 2004). Meanwhile, student fees at English universities have increased dramatically. So much for access.

The technical rationality that steers instructional design in the context of standardized course packaging and technology adoption (e.g. competency-based instruction) serves the system from the standpoint of curriculum management. And while curriculum formats that exemplify this standpoint are favoured because they require measurable objectives, they have not been shown over the years to achieve their aims in terms of actual performance (i.e. in terms of practical achievements in literacy, professional work and so on). Of greater significance is how these curriculum formats, so readily amenable to standardized packaging and online learning, operate to (mis)shape the learning contexts on which they are imposed.

These concerns about the pervasive distorting effects of technical rationality in curriculum design (i.e. the obsession with technique and with the deployment of the very latest technology) are still relevant if we look generally at curriculum design and implementation practices. However, recent publications on technology adoption in education, particularly in e-learning, tend to dissociate themselves from the elevation of instructional design approaches derived from an obsession with technique. A recent, well-researched text by Roblyer *et al.* (2002), provides 'realistic examples, tips and exercises to demonstrate how technology can be used as a tool for learning'. The editors stress that 'good teaching comes first', placing it at the head of their list of 'values that should underlie our use of technology in education' (p. xvii). Yet their 'teaching comes first' mantra is a prelude to the book's primary interest in harnessing technology adoption to teaching and learning in the academy. Further, their claim that 'we control how the media is used in education' (p. xviii) is problematic. Too much emphasis is placed unrealistically on the agency of the educators and too little on those media effects that cannot be so readily integrated into curriculum development. For all the heartfelt emphasis at the beginning of the text on the practical art of teaching, technical rationality is pervasive throughout. Concern for the integration of technology is its major theme and the role (agency) of the teacher in shaping the learning context is accordingly reduced.

Similarly, adult educator and instructional designer Dirk Morrison confronts 'the imperative pre-requisite to the effective adoption of e-learning in higher education' and 'the need for a new pedagogy' (2006: 104) that this imperative prefigures. Morrison concludes that there is a 'need to create learning environments that require the development of critical, creative and complex thinking skills' (p. 116). He argues convincingly that prevailing instructional strategies are no longer appropriate. While there is still a strong sense in his call of an over-determined preoccupation with technology adoption, Morrison's arguments imply a need to assess the relevance of the entire discourse of curriculum design, including the inordinately heavy emphasis on curriculum methods courses in teacher training. Such an assessment should act as a prelude to transforming the goals of colleges of education.

Critical observations on how administrators in postsecondary education are falling short in their understanding of technology adoption merit further analysis. And especially so if using an adult education standpoint that has always placed a high value on distance learning and still takes into account the experience adult learners bring to the situation. From the beginnings of the UK Mechanics' Institutes movement in the 1820s, the conviction that the education of a free people should ultimately be in their own hands (Collins

1998: 136) has guided the emancipatory practice of adult education, mainly expressed nowadays through the pedagogy of Paulo Freire. We might want to use this viewpoint to consider a hopeful pedagogy that envisages how new developments via the internet (aside from the professionalized concerns about adoption and deployment) are opening up prospects for learning – increasingly for ordinary learners. The advent of internet developments such as iPod and YouTube places the tempo and pedagogical content in the hands of these learners, confirming that authentic ways of knowing emanate from individual and collective action in community; in effect a form of 'digital democracy' (see *Time*, 25 December 2006/1 January 2007: 16) that creates huge changes in ways of knowing, self-expression and relationships (Tapscott and Williams 2007). Access to a surfeit of information beyond what Google provides, and the re-casting of learners as producers engaging with learner-produced materials, undermine the traditional dissemination-of-information approach to curriculum design. Eventually, it is reasonable to speculate, the long-term viability of lock-step, credit-accumulation degree programmes might be threatened. In such scenarios, even enlightened educators bent on systematically integrating technology into teaching practice and mediating institutional e-learning might see the development of learning potential through a rear-view mirror.

Postsecondary institutions, given their legitimate status, have time for adjustment to the consequences of rapidly increasing access to communications technology. University administrators, for example, can frame more credible responses to widespread plagiarism. No doubt the pseudo-ethical and legalistic terms in which university administrators express their fretful responses to student (mis)application of ready-made, online academic essays will persist until educators address realistically the transformation of curriculum and programme development. In the meantime, adult educators on and off campus are well positioned ethically and strategically to generate a discourse from the standpoint of community interests – to recognize the growing feasibility of knowledge production on behalf of ordinary men and women and the right to ready access to publicly-funded educational institutions. But I expect a tendency for university interests to set the discourse agenda. The challenge for concerned educators and community activists is to re-shape the corporate university agenda in the face of campus restructuring that moves university attention away from public service extension (extramural) activities to market model enterprise initiatives, to the use of public funds to advance private sector interests, and to the continuing escalation of student fees.

Conclusion

Web-connected technological innovations such as the cell-phone, iPod and YouTube are altering individual and social learning processes in complex ways that merit careful investigation by educators committed to distance learning. The potential of this emerging communications technology to enhance individual and collective learning prefigures radical changes in how educators approach curricula.

These developments endorse the observations made by the pioneers about the need to always place the interests of learners and teachers above any preoccupation with technology deployment. In any case, for better or worse, that deployment carries a momentum all of its own.

At the level of the system, the moves into online learning in higher education are now more appropriately examined within a learning context that focuses sharply on the development of critical thought (Morrison 2006: 104). In a sense (and e-learning aside) this emphasis on engendering critical thought and 'deep thinking' entails looking backwards to the future. Educators already morally committed to distance learning, to learners such as Rita, and to the legacy of the pioneers in this book (as well as Jennie Lee and Walter Perry) now have a critical role to play in reclaiming our publicly-funded higher education institutions for non-profit-generating community service. The founding intentions of distance education to provide wider access and to sustain the ideal of education as a public good (rather than an exploitable source of private profit) call for a renewed consciousness among academics and teachers, as intellectuals, of their social responsibility to the wider community. In the light of its higher ideals, distance education is virtually compelled to question the system and to challenge a conventional reality imposed by marketplace imperatives.

References

Atthill, C. (2001) Towards ethical distance education? *Open Learning*, 16(1): 85–7.

Clark, B. (ed.) (2001) *Creating Entrepreneurial Universities: Organizational Pathways of Transformation.* Oxford: Pergamon Press.

Collins, M. (1991) *Adult Education as Vocation: A Critical Role for the Adult Educator.* New York: Routledge.

Collins, M. (1998) *Critical Crosscurrents in Education.* Malabar, FL: Krieger.

Currie, J.K. and Newson, J. (eds) (1998) *Universities and Globalization: Critical Perspectives.* Thousand Oaks, CA.: Sage.

Freire, P. (1981) *Pedagogy of the Oppressed.* New York: Continuum.

Katz, J.E. and Aakhus, M. (2002) *Perpetual Contact: Mobile Communication, Private Talk, Public Performance.* Cambridge: Cambridge University Press.

MacLeod, D. (2004) Hefce pulls the plug on UK e-university, *Guardian*, 4 March.

McLuhan, M. (1967) *The Medium is the Message.* New York: Bantam.

Mezirow, J. (1995) Transformation theory of adult learning, in M. Welton (ed.) *In Defense of the Lifeworld: Critical Perspectives on Adult Learning.* Albany, NY: State University of New York Press.

Morrison, D. (2006) E-learning in higher education: the need for a new pedagogy, in M. Bullen and D.P. Janes (eds) *Making the Transition to E-learning: Strategies and Issues.* London: Information Science Publishing.

Perry, W. (1976) *Open University: A Personal Account.* Milton Keynes: Open University Press.

Roblyer, M., Edwards, J. and Schwier, R. (eds) (2002) *Integrating Educational Technology into Teaching* (Canadian edition). Toronto: Pearson Education Canada.

Rogers, E.M. (2003) *Diffusion of Innovations*, 5th edn. New York: The Free Press.

Sumner, J. (2000) Serving the system: a critical history of distance education, *Open Learning*, 15(3): 26–85.

Tapscott, D. and Williams, A.D. (2007) *Wikinomics: How Mass Collaboration Changes Everything*. New York: Portfolio, Penguin.

von Prümmer, C. (2000) *Women and Distance Education*. London: Routledge.

Welton, M. (1993) The contribution of critical theory to our understanding of adult learning, in S. Merriam (ed.) *An Update on Adult Learning Theory*. San Francisco: Jossey-Bass.

Welton, M. (ed.) (1995) *In Defense of the Lifeworld*. Albany, NY: State University of New York Press.

Woodhouse, H. (2001) The market model of education and the threat to Canadian universities, *Encounters on Education*, 2: 105–22.

8

Some experiences of a distance educator

Sir John Daniel

Familiar territory

Reading the interview summaries in the earlier part of this book was like
walking through familiar territory in comfortable shoes. Two-thirds of the
interviewees are friends and I have met most of the others. I reflected that
either Liz had recruited her experts from a limited pool or I am better
networked than I thought. In fact both are true. First, she consciously chose
distance learning practitioners at or nearing retirement – those of us who
had the good fortune to be loitering near the bottom step of the escalator of
distance education when it started to move upwards.

Second, we are a remarkably well-networked group because, as Ian
Mugridge remarks in Chapter 3, there was so little public-sector distance education in the 1970s that we had to huddle together for warmth in international
conferences for professional sustenance.

My brief is to react to the interview chapters and give advice to younger
practitioners and researchers on fruitful paths to follow. I shall respond in
an integrated way, rooting the advice in my own personal experience and
convictions.

Conversion on the road to Milton Keynes

I found distance education while seeking something else. My first real
job, after a long and conventional education, was an assistant professorship
of metallurgical engineering at the Ecole Polytechnique (Université de
Montréal). Fate appeared to have made me a university teacher so I thought
I ought to develop some professionalism in my new *métier* by undertaking
formal study of education. Before I realized that this was an unusual – even
perverse – reflex for a young engineering academic, I had enrolled in a masters programme in educational technology at Sir George Williams University
(now Concordia University). I had little idea what educational technology

was but swallowed my scepticism because it was the only programme in Montreal with 'education' in the title that could be studied part-time and appeared to offer some intellectual challenge.

For someone who had specialized in science for many years the whole programme was an eye-opener, but its three-month internship changed my life. As I wondered in 1971 where to go for my internship the press was suddenly full of stories about an amazing innovation – by the Brits of all people – called the Open University. It sounded interesting and Professor David Hawkridge took me on as an unpaid visiting lecturer at the Open University's Institute of Educational Technology for the summer of 1972. I did no lecturing but I had a conversion experience.

I was introduced to the practice of developing courses in teams, which the founding vice-chancellor of the Open University, Walter Perry, regarded as his major innovation. I was a back-row player in a science course, 'Solids, liquids and gases', which later acquired a reputation as one of the Open University's few 'dogs'. Much more interesting was my larger role in a team charged with proposing revisions to the technology foundation course, T100, then being offered for the first time. I had to sift through the abundant information that the Open University collects from its students and suggest changes that would improve the course the following year.

I found this systematic approach to quality improvement inspiring, as I did everything else about that summer. I spent all my spare moments viewing Open University TV programmes and was amazed by their quality and interest. I went along to a residential summer school and was bowled over by the 16-hour-a-day commitment to academic discourse: in labs and field trips during the day and in the bar until late at night. The idealism and the commitment to student success were palpable.

Here was a teaching and learning *system*. When my internship ended I was no longer at ease in the old dispensation. Here was the future of higher education and I wanted to be part of it.

> **Advice:** *If you hear of a new development that sounds interesting and important, try to go to the source and learn more about it.*

On returning to Montreal an opportunity to join the distance learning revolution came almost immediately in the form of an advertisement in *Le Devoir* seeking a director-general for the new Télé-université; Quebec's answer to the UK Open University. With youthful enthusiasm I applied for the job, even though I was an Anglophone, barely 30 years old, who had only stepped off the boat from Europe three years earlier.

To their eternal credit the search committee, instead of binning my application, called me up to Quebec City for interview. They made it clear that they were not going to make me director-general – which was a relief – but told me that I was the only person they could find in Quebec who had seen an open university from the inside. Would I like to join the Télé-université and organize its educational technology unit? I replied that I would!

Advice: If you want to make a career change – don't be bashful!

Improvement by feedback

We moved from Montreal to Quebec City and had four tremendously stimulating years – both professionally and personally. The UK Open University had its well-staffed Institute of Educational Technology; the Télé-université had me! How could I make an impact? I decided that evaluating our first course offerings and feeding back the results to the course teams was the most fruitful approach. It did not make me popular, because even the innovators and risk-takers who had joined the Télé-université did not like to be told that students did not find their work perfect. However, the institution steadily became a self-improving system.

The years at the Télé-université were intensely interesting on the personal front because, as a new institution using media to reach large numbers, it was a magnet for the young nationalist academics who wanted to promote change by spicing the traditional academic fare of Quebec social science with more penetrating insights. They were splendid people whose commitment to the sovereignty of Quebec was more than rhetorical. In the election of 1976, which swept the *Parti Québecois* to power as the provincial government, four of my faculty (by then I had become director of studies) were elected to the National Assembly and three of them immediately became ministers.

Advice: Don't be afraid to take a flyer on a new opportunity. It may enrich you personally as well as professionally.

During these years I attended my first international conference on distance learning, the 1975 conference of the International Council for Correspondence Education (ICCE), held in Brighton, UK. At that time ICCE's membership was a blend of commercial, military and public sector correspondence schools. Walter Perry was the star turn of the meeting with a speech about the Open University. In his uncompromising way Perry said bluntly that the Open University was providing the quality learning material and student support so lacking in the correspondence sector. By the end of the conference the battle lines were drawn. The public-sector university people were feeling superior. The commercial schools were arguing that with generous public funding, they too could offer exciting media and excellent student support.

Research: There is some interesting research to be done on the role of professional associations such as ICCE/ICDE; EDEN; AAOU, etc. in furthering practice and defining the field of open distance learning.

Improvement by clarity

By now open university networks were forming. Alberta had created Athabasca University (AU) as Quebec set up the Télé-université. There was contact between the institutions and we worked together on evaluating the first educational experiments conducted on Canada's communications satellites.

One thing led to another and in 1977, in the depths of the cold Alberta winter, I arrived in Edmonton to take up the post of vice-president, learning services, at AU. AU had originally been established as an overspill campus to the University of Alberta, but as that became less necessary and scandal erupted over land sales near the campus site, it sought a new mission as an open university.

It had produced one blockbuster course: 'Ancient roots of the modern world', which required 19 3000-word assignments and should have led to the award of a full degree, rather than a few course credits, for any student courageous enough to get through it. (My wife and I later took the course as students in a slimmed-down version and found it excellent.)

> **Advice:** *Enrol as a student in courses offered by your institution. It is good lifelong learning and the best way of finding out in a holistic manner how well you serve your students.*

When I arrived, AU was still trying to find its way to a fuller curriculum. However, each successive meeting of the senate jettisoned the course and programme proposals approved at the previous meeting and set off in a new direction. Taking the view that implementing an imperfect programme consistently was more productive than an endless search for a perfect curriculum, I simply insisted that we develop the courses that had been agreed. Once they recovered from their surprise my colleagues thought this was an excellent idea and set to work with a will. Enrolments doubled in each of the three years that I was there.

My stay was short because Sam Smith, AU's president who had lured me west, fancied himself as a kingmaker. Suggesting to me that after six years in unorthodox open-university start-ups it was time to establish my credentials in the conventional sector, he placed before me an advertisement for the post of vice-rector, academic, at Concordia University. Being an obedient type I took his advice, applied and got the job.

> **Advice:** *Listen to others' advice and don't be afraid to take detours.*

Appointing me was broadminded on Concordia's part because at that stage I was a drop-out from the masters programme in educational technology that I had started at Sir George Williams University in 1970. I had completed the coursework and the internship but had abandoned a research thesis on the introduction of computers in Quebec primary schools when I moved to Alberta. (Sir George Williams University and Loyola College had merged to form Concordia in 1974.)

Concordia gave me a wonderful training in every aspect of conventional university management under the wise guidance of Rector John O'Brien. The university did not teach at a distance but my involvement with open distance learning continued through ICCE.

ICCE had held another conference in New Delhi in 1978 at which I was elected chairman of the programme committee for the 1982 conference scheduled for Vancouver. Then in 1979 the Open University (UK) held a memorable invitational conference to celebrate its tenth anniversary. Whether to create an international association of open universities was one of the issues discussed.

David Sewart of the UK Open University had been active at both the Brighton and New Delhi ICCE conferences. He and I thought that it would be better to expand the remit of ICCE to include the interests of the open universities rather than create a new association for them. Discussion at the UK Open University conference already indicated that drafting the membership criteria for such an association would be difficult.

At this time the growing professional community of public-sector distance education was increasingly uncomfortable with the designation 'correspondence education'. On the one hand it did not capture the richness of the new multimedia approaches and on the other it had unfortunate associations with dubious courses advertised on packets of matches. Changing the name of the International Council for Correspondence Education was a *sine qua non* for broadening its membership base.

With the strong support of Kevin Smith of the University of New England (Australia), David Sewart and I began a campaign to change 'correspondence' to 'distance' to convert ICCE to ICDE. This was put to a vote at the Vancouver conference and approved. Sadly, however, the commercial correspondence sector interpreted this as a repudiation of their interests and gradually drifted away from ICDE, causing its membership to focus more on higher education and the public sector than before.

> **Advice:** *Don't be afraid to initiate reforms, but don't be surprised if they have unintended consequences.*

> **Research:** *The terminology of distance education is a rich field of study because our field has a lamentable tendency to invent new names for what we do without properly defining them: for example, flexible learning, blended learning, e-learning, virtual learning, online learning, distributed learning, etc.*

At the Vancouver conference I was elected president of ICDE and used some of the surplus generated by the event to convene face-to-face meetings of the executive committee and promote the Council around the world. Unfortunately subsequent conferences did not generate surpluses and ICDE gradually became more dependent on government grants, diminishing its credibility as the membership gradually ceded control of the association to the secretariat. The Asian Association of Open Universities emerged in the 1990s as the most stimulating forum for discussions of open distance learning.

The challenge of dual-mode operation

Before the ICDE met again for its Melbourne Conference in 1985 I had moved again, to the presidency of Laurentian University, a multi-campus institution serving north-eastern Ontario from its main campus in Sudbury.

This brought me back into direct operational contact with open distance learning since Laurentian is dual-mode institution. Watching the faculty struggle – or fail to struggle – to serve both their on-campus and off-campus students gave me a conviction, which has never left me, that managing dual-mode operations is extremely difficult. Whatever arrangements are put in place seem inherently unstable. Too much centralization of the organization of distance learning and the faculty feel disempowered; too much delegation of responsibility for distance learning to individual academics and student support becomes inconsistent.

Some would say that the blending of distance and classroom learning through e-learning has made this distinction irrelevant. That may be true but dual-mode e-learning raises another fundamental question. Does not the cottage industry approach to e-learning through dual-mode operation effectively ensure that this powerful new teaching tool performs below potential?

Those who believe that expanding access is a fundamental mission of distance learning should also worry that e-learning is diverting attention and resources away from disadvantaged students and back to those who are already well served. For example, the Sloan Foundation's interesting annual reports on e-learning in the USA (Allen and Seaman 2006) explicitly duck the question of whether the e-learners are new students. Is e-learning just another example of the empire striking back, with traditional academe undermining attempts to widen access?

> **Research:** *We need more research on e-learning and dual-mode operations by dispassionate investigators without a vested interest in the results.*

> **Advice:** *Young practitioners of distance learning should follow closely the research on e-learning, m-learning (mobile learning) and other new technologies so that they can use them for maximum benefit to students.*

Open distance learning on the international agenda

At Laurentian my extracurricular activities within the Canadian Association of Distance Education and the Canadian Higher Education Research Network gave me a good overview of developments across Canada. In 1987 Prime Minister Brian Mulroney hosted both the Commonwealth Heads of Government Meeting (CHOGM) and the Sommet de la Francophonie. He intended to propose initiatives for the educational use of communication technologies to both gatherings and I was drawn into an informal group led by Canada's Department of Communications that advised on the presentation to the Commonwealth.

At the CHOGM, which was held in Vancouver, Mulroney's proposal was reviewed alongside a report from a group led by Lord Asa Briggs: *Towards a Commonwealth of Learning*. This had grown out of the work of the Commonwealth Standing Committee on Student Mobility which, worried by impact of rising fees on the numbers of students from developing countries going overseas to study, wondered if modern technology could make it possible to move the courses rather than the students.

The upshot was a decision by the heads of government to create the Commonwealth of Learning (COL). The UK's Margaret Thatcher was opposed to the creation of another intergovernmental body but India's Rajiv Gandhi supported it strongly and pledged a hard currency contribution, as did Brunei and Nigeria, so the developing world won the day. Exactly what the COL would be or do was left for later decision.

Shortly afterwards I was asked to chair a planning committee to put flesh on the bones of COL. We worked through 1988 and produced a memorandum of understanding that governments signed later in the year.

The fundamental question before the planning committee was whether COL would produce courses and offer them to Commonwealth countries through technologies such as satellites, or help countries to build up their own capacity for distance education. The committee chose the second option, strongly influenced by the international development agencies of Australia, Canada and the UK. These agencies were to provide funding for COL and experience had made them sceptical about hi-tech educational systems for developing countries. In the initial years the UK, reflecting Margaret Thatcher's scepticism about COL, supported it by funding services from the UK Open University rather than by transferring funds to Vancouver, which had been chosen as the home of the organization. As chairman I joined the other members of the planning committee in expressing disappointment with the UK's unilateral stance.

Open as to people, places, methods and ideas

This proved ironic because in 1989, when on leave from Laurentian at a senior executive course in international affairs at the National Defence College of Canada, I was appointed vice-chancellor of the UK Open University. On taking up the post in 1990 I found myself in receipt of the funds for supporting COL that I earlier thought should have gone directly to Vancouver!

> **Advice:** *Always be courteous when criticizing others' actions. Institutional loyalties may later cause you to eat your words.*

The UK Open University is an extraordinary institution – certainly among the most successful new organizations created in the twentieth century – and leading it for 11 years was a thrilling task. Eighteen years earlier I had been an unpaid intern; now I had the top job. Such has been the numerical impact of the Open University, and such the satisfaction it gives its students, that wherever I gave speeches, all over the world, people would pop up in the audience with warm testimonials to the quality of the institution.

The situation that I found at the Open University on arrival in 1990 was almost the opposite of the challenge that faced me at Athabasca a dozen years earlier. The Open University was brilliant at consistent organizational follow-through but its self-confidence had suffered through political vicissitudes in the late 1980s. My new colleagues were deeply suspicious of an imminent government review of its funding.

Being able to make international comparisons, I was perhaps more aware than they of the remarkable quality and value for money that the Open University represented, so I insisted that we work openly and collaboratively with the review. We later discovered that the real purpose of the review was to help government decide how to position the Open University in the major reform of UK higher education that was coming in 1992. This positioning proved highly favourable. First, the Open University became effectively the only national university in a newly-federal structure. Second, the creation of common funding and quality assurance mechanisms for all UK universities enabled the Open University to leverage its cost-effectiveness and quality into a doubling of enrolments over the 1990s and a steady rise to fifth place in national rankings of teaching quality in the country's hundred universities by the early 2000s.

Advice: If you have a good story to tell, don't fear outside scrutiny.

As part of my strategy of strengthening the Open University's faith in its mandate and capabilities I reminded colleagues relentlessly of the inspiring mission articulated by its first chancellor, Lord Crowther: to be open as to people, open as to places, open as to methods and open as to ideas. Fidelity to this mission led the university to grow in numbers, to extend its reach to the rest of Europe and beyond, to embrace the online world, and to lead higher education in the adoption of concepts such as foundation degrees and national vocational qualifications.

In a highly effective and well-governed institution like the Open University, an important role for the leadership is to create room and resources for new initiatives that lack natural constituencies of support among the established faculties and schools. In this respect my riskiest decision was to persuade the Council in 1995 to invest about US $25 million (or GBP 15 million) in fully embracing the internet. Fortunately it paid excellent dividends as the faculties responded with enthusiasm and the Knowledge Media Institute, which was created as part of the package, rapidly acquired an international reputation. This meant that when the dotcom frenzy struck in 2000 the university was already exploiting online technology in a big way.

A decision that my successor came to regret was our establishment of the United States Open University in the late 1990s. The UK Open University Council closed it in 2002 because by then the financial outlay and the time required to bring it to break-even were both too great for comfort for a public sector institution.

The interesting question is whether the US operation could have been brought to success if the UK Open University had been in the private rather than the public sector. This touches on a wider interrogation about the profile of distance education in the future. I was lucky to begin a fascinating career just as the public sector displaced the private sector as the locus of the exciting developments in distance learning. As my career draws to a close I suspect that the private sector is returning to the ascendant. Certainly private institutions will play a major role in the development of higher education in developing countries (Daniel *et al.* 2006) and some are gearing up to do this through distance learning.

> **Advice:** *Anyone contemplating a career in distancce learning in the twenty-first century should consider joining the private sector, which may see more exciting action.*

Early in my time at the UK Open University I completed the courses for a diploma in theology by distance learning that I had begun at Laurentian. Wishing to continue as a distance learner, I was about to enrol in a law programme when my exasperated wife sat me down and told me firmly that if I wanted to be a student again I should finish the educational technology masters degree that I had begun two decades earlier.

Concordia University, showing admirable broadmindedness once again, let me back in to the programme and the UK Open University gave me a month's study leave. In a month in Montreal, which coincided exactly with the 1995 referendum campaign on Quebec sovereignty, I coined the term 'mega-universities' and wrote a thesis about them which became my book *Mega-universities and Knowledge Media: Technology Strategies for Higher Education*, published in 1996, 25 years after I had started the programme. At that time I officiated at a dozen UK Open University degree ceremonies each year and was able to comfort, by citing my own experience, graduates who felt they had taken too long to complete.

> **Advice:** *Lifelong learning is just that. Don't be afraid to take your time.*

Distance education for development

In 2001 my career took a new turn when I joined UNESCO as head of education. This took me away from distance education but plunged me into the challenges of education in the developing world. Job number one at UNESCO, then as now, was to help the world achieve education for all. I took my second UK Open University course, 'Third World development', in order to learn more about it.

> **Advice:** *Don't be afraid to get the job first and then qualify for it!*

UNESCO was fascinating and I learned much about how intergovernmental agencies work while assisting Director-General Matsuura in his attempts to reform an idealistic but somewhat dysfunctional organization. This experience was invaluable when another wheel came full circle in 2004 and I became president of the COL, the small intergovernmental agency that I had helped to plan in 1988. For me this is the perfect job, combining as it does distance education, international development and institutional leadership. COL operates from the principles that development in all fields is largely a matter of learning; that traditional teaching methods cannot cope with the scale of the challenge; and that technology-mediated learning and distance learning are a large part of the answer.

This is not the place to go into detail about COL's work, which is described from many angles in my speeches (www.col.org/speeches). Suffice it to say that a small but extraordinarily talented staff of only 40 punch far above their weight in helping the developing countries of the Commonwealth to develop policies, systems, models and materials for expanding and improving learning through technology.

Conclusion

By following the thread of distance education wherever it led me I have been blessed with a thoroughly engaging and enjoyable career. Those beginning a career in the field today will face fresh challenges and different opportunities. My final advice to our young successors is fourfold. First, be clear about the values that underpin your work. Second, pay less attention to technology, which will continue to evolve, than to new ways of doing things. For my generation the great innovation was the course team. For the next I suspect that it will be open educational resources (OERs). Research in how best to convert OERs to credit-bearing courses will repay dividends.

Third, be alert to developments in both the public and private sectors, which are moving closer together. Finally, I urge you to follow your own convictions without worrying too much about what others think. A constant feature of my own professional trajectory was that whenever I moved on, colleagues at the institution I was leaving thought I was mad and warned me against putting my career at risk and my happiness in jeopardy. They were all proved wrong!

References

Allen, I.E. and Seaman, J. (2006) *Making the Grade: Online Education in the United States.* Needham, MA: Sloan Consortium.

Daniel, J.S. (1996) *Mega-universities and Knowledge Media: Technology Strategies for Higher Education.* London: Kogan Page.

Daniel, J.S., Kanwar, A. and Uvalic-Trumbic, S. (2006) A tectonic shift in higher education? *Change Magazine,* July/August 38(4): 16–23.

9

Passionate pioneers

Yvonne Hillier

I was flattered, surprised and excited to be asked to write a chapter for this book. I was asked to react, based on my own experience, to the findings presented. There were two guiding questions to help structure my response: what could less experienced practitioners and researchers consider and what might promote theory-building or practice enhancement for postsecondary education?

I began reading through the first chapter and was immediately struck by how powerful the language was. I also realized that I was responding to the practitioner accounts with excitement. The words of the participants had been my experiences, too, in a different field: adult literacy, language and numeracy (ALLN). ALLN, too, had to evolve out of nothing. I could see parallels which were so strong that I sensed there was something about working in a new field that required certain key factors to help establish it for future successful practice. I have been part of a field which had to establish its credibility, to fight for resources, to ask basic questions about what we were doing and why, and all the while being aware that I was part of something creative, challenging but so, so important that at times I was an evangelist for my work. This chapter is informed by my own experiences in this different, yet similar, field and relates it to my growing understanding of what it means to be a professional in postcompulsory education.

I have drawn upon recent work that my friend and colleague, Professor Mary Hamilton and I have published on the history of ALLN and in particular, on deliberative policy analysis (DPA), drawing on the work of Hajer and Wagenaar (2003). Hajer and Wagenaar recognize that there are multiple actors with different investments and resources in any field. They argue that people's engagement in policy enactment is:

> fuelled and expressed in their passions and feelings about certain situations. They harbour sympathies and antipathies toward the people that

make up their world. They are strongly committed to some subjects and indifferent and apathetic towards others.

(2003: 21)

Hajer and Wagenaar assert that people who are involved on a day-to-day basis with any particular problem are highly knowledgeable about their situation and need to be included in the policy-making process in a much more open and democratic way than traditional top-down policy-making allows. Decisions and networks outside formal institutions can be an important part of determining the policy process. DPA takes *practices* as its unit of analysis. Its task, Hajer and Wagenaar argue, is to reveal the hidden ambiguity and uncertainties in the taken-for-granted policy practices and discourse with the purpose of creating reflexive space for deliberation of issues. This space contributes to the policy process appropriate to current conditions that hold within our networked society. Organizational culture is important to consider in this process, though hard to manage since unpredictable meanings and interpretations are involved.

Using DPA, Mary and I suggested that there are five lenses that we can apply to the analysis of the field of ALLN: chronology, discourse, agency, tension and deliberative spaces (Hamilton and Hillier 2006). After reading the findings in this book I could see that although we had applied this analysis to our field of ALLN, which had developed from the mid-1970s, the development of distance learning had followed similar trajectories. I am powerfully struck by how the stories in this book can also be examined using these lenses and I want to focus in particular on three of them: discourse, agency and tension.

Stories of engagement

Discourse

One of the helpful ways to read practitioners' accounts is to search for the discourses they employ. It was easy to spot some of the metaphors they used to describe how they joined and then remained in the new field of distance learning. In the first chapter, participants discuss their excitement, their passion and sense of mission through such words as 'evangelical religion' and statements such as 'YES, this is what education is really about'. Interestingly, Liz also employed this discourse when she portrayed the participants. By the end of Chapter 1, we have read that they are passionate, they have boldly gone into unmapped and difficult territories and they have created extraordinary learning opportunities for millions of adults. The metaphor of exploration, going into new territory as pioneers, breaking new ground and laying down foundations for future generations of practitioners is a powerful way to describe the evolving field. Practitioners talk about 'being in the dark' when they started. Indeed, in a new field of practice, how can pioneers know what challenges and opportunities lie before them when they do not yet know what kind of terrain they have to navigate?

When we look at how practitioners describe their initial involvement with distance learning, we see that they have already got strategies. For some, this is at a practical level and for others it is more strategic. The metaphor that arises from the description of how they managed this is again strong but here enthusiasm is replaced by something more serious. This brings me to a second metaphor. Throughout the stories, we read how people have acted to develop and also protect what they believe in. Liz describes this in terms of 'battlefields' and 'conflictual situations'. One practitioner argued the need to fight to protect the field, another mentions 'downright hostility'. At the same time, there are accounts of 'innocence' and having no rules to play by. My sense is that participants have employed the stronger metaphors of fighting but need to moderate this, given their educational cultures, into something less severe. In fact, participants' actions and their understanding of these lead me to the next lens to examine their stories by, individual agency.

Agency

Agency relates to people's actions in the world but it cannot be divorced from structure, or the environment within which people live. There is a complex interaction between individual agency and management which relates to institutional structures. An interesting question to ask of the accounts of early engagement in the emerging field is how individual practitioners managed to gain authority and respect for distance learning. There was lack of knowledge of how best to develop distance learning and self-acknowledged helplessness, 'blundering around in the dark' and 'making it up as we went along'. Yet from this, practitioners have obviously developed knowledge and experience which informed their understanding – in other words, their informal theories of what to do.

I have a profound sense of what people believe in from the stories told in this book. The practitioners convey the notion that there is potential inherent in everyone, that they want to provide a 'service' to learners, they want to make a difference in their lives, and these beliefs all appear to stem from a deeply-held commitment to social justice. To help achieve these goals is the idea that folk should 'never give up' and that there is 'always a new chance after every disaster', and of course, if all else fails, there is influence by 'stealth'!

I can see that the early pioneers understood quite a lot about how to achieve things. They worked collaboratively with like-minded folk, building alliances. They understood that they should use their own 'common sense', which I would interpret as their informal, practitioner theories (see Hillier 2006). They understood that they needed to experiment; again, not words they used, but I would argue they were testing out their informal theories, or as one participant observed, 'trying things and seeing what worked'.

One practitioner describes being able to take risks but having a 'safety net'. I enjoyed the tip from another practitioner that it was important, despite feeling that everything was new and therefore not quite legitimate with traditionalists, to nonetheless let others think that 'you knew what you were talking about!' It was interesting, too, to read about people's convictions, that they *knew* something was right or that it guided their practice which was then later tested and provided evidence for their initial beliefs.

Autonomy

One of the participant characteristics that experienced practitioners seem to have shared in the early years was autonomy. They *could* try things out, they *could* make it up, they *could* create new practices. They *could* be strategic, political and subversive, ranging from knowing about allies to knowing about the 'opposition'. Words such as 'champions' and 'charismatic individuals' demonstrate how much people and the action that they can take will influence the direction of an emerging field as well as 'keeping their gunpowder dry' and being politically astute.

Autonomy is an important contributing factor in effective individual agency. I suggest that a newly emerging field can benefit by how much autonomy practitioners have. One of the worrying constraints on our current situation in England in particular is the degree to which practitioners have to comply with the national qualifications framework. They have to abide by a national curriculum and evidence of learning is only accepted through learners gaining achievements on national tests. The funding mechanism, too, directs institutional behaviour towards recruiting and retaining learners so that they can also benefit from funds held back for their achievements. Although this has not yet permeated into the funding mechanism of higher education, quality assurance indicators take account of retention and student numbers are agreed on the basis of past institutional performance. The role of individuals and their levels of autonomy have been particularly squeezed in this compliant culture.

I was also struck by how participants, although they felt frightened, were having *fun*. I suspect that having no rules and being able to create new practices is so enjoyable that the realization that people were moving into unknown territory was more exciting than scary. How many opportunities are there today to do this? The challenging factor for today's newer entrants to the field is how the current climate of institution-based compliance, control and competitiveness severely constrains the opportunities for autonomy and experimentation and sadly reduces opportunities to be creative and to enjoy the fun that this affords.

Tension

Inevitably, where folk are forging new practices there will be disagreements. These range from those at institutional level, where funding and resourcing for new materials and staffing structures have to be identified and agreed, to fostering new approaches to teaching and learning and having these accepted by tutors and learners alike. It was unsurprising, therefore, to read of these. My third lens, tension, provides a framework for analysis. This lens links, though, with the lens of agency. People who are experiencing tension can respond in various ways, through denial or through overt confrontation, but in these stories there seems to be an underpinning commitment to 'making it work'. Such a commitment helps to manage the tensions and, in some cases, reduce them. This is an effective strategy and one that many authors of change management would recognize – that is, to encourage people to own the need for change and then together identify strategies to enable this to happen.

Tensions do not just arise from differences of opinion about how best to foster learning at a distance. Any new field has to establish its credibility and given that practitioners did have opportunities to create new practices from scratch, the lack of prior *legitimized* practical knowledge can threaten existing practices. What is interesting, particularly in the UK context, is that some of the new practices have become so successful that they are now in the mainstream of teaching and learning and offered as good practice. I am thinking particularly of the good work of the Open University (UK), where approaches to assessment and providing feedback to learners that tutors may or may not see face to face have sharpened the practice of tutors in more traditional classroom-based settings. These practices have been achieved, though, through management of tensions such as requiring highly autonomous lecturers in higher education to discuss more openly and change their approaches to assessment, all the while scrutinized by a quality assurance mechanism.

Recent moves to 'encourage' staff in institutions to engage with virtual learning environments (VLEs) bring to the fore tensions regarding the exploration of innovative ways to foster learning against being forced to use these means to teach even more students at lower cost. The latter, interestingly, is never the case and many practitioners now find themselves prisoners of emails, discussion boards and expectations for immediate responses to student communication.

The findings indicate an uncomfortable intersection of unreflective habit and unsought change in traditional institutions which the development of distance learning had to challenge. There is the 'classic divide' between snobbery and innovation. There is also the difficulty in keeping a balance between idealistic approaches to this new field and the need to be pragmatic, perhaps in limiting the content of new 'packages' or realizing that not all tutors will adopt the developing teaching and learning strategies fostered by distance learning. There are the inevitable tensions concerning the management of limited resources and the imposition of top-down management imperatives. There is the drive for respectability and the practical need for feasibility.

Theory-building and practice enhancement

Deliberative spaces

What does my application of the DPA framework mean for our understanding of distance learning? My argument is that applying the lenses of discourse, agency and tension to distance learning enables us to monitor and shape its development. To do this requires the fourth lens, deliberative spaces, defined by Hamilton and Hillier as 'the availability and distribution of deliberative, reflexive space to engage with issues' (2006: 42). Through this lens we ask, what spaces for such discussion, reflection and action exist over time and how do people move into these spaces? The participants in this book have at times been able to use structures in their higher education and postcompulsory systems to shape their field. Their stories show how they have helped to 'shape, grasp and legitimate' the actions and the situations that gave rise to them (Hajer and Wagenaar 2003: 156). They have particularly been able to make use of technology, to keep pace with new developments, create networks and disseminate good practice.

Deliberative spaces are an important factor in enabling practice to develop. What spaces for discussion, reflection and action have been available to people at different points in their engagement with distance learning? What, in today's time-short, often stressful workplaces, is the availability and distribution of deliberative, reflexive space to engage with the issues Liz has identified?

In ALLN, the spaces occupied by practitioners in the early years of informal groups who came together to help publish student writing or create learning resources have long gone. More formal spaces created through the national agency (now the Basic Skills Agency) to fund practitioner-led development have also disappeared and been replaced by government-sponsored professional development programmes to ensure that staff in the field are qualified to meet the national Skills for Life Strategy. There are, though, opportunities for people to meet through alternative networks such as the Research and Practice in Adult Literacy (RaPAL) which continues to draw interest from practitioners and providers across the UK.

What actions can people undertake when deliberative space is absent? How can future practitioners ensure that they maintain the deliberative spaces they have or argue for these where they do not exist? How might future practitioners even regard the need for reflective space, particularly when they are so bombarded with opportunities to network in more superficial ways through electronic discussion groups and forums? These are important questions for the field and provide markers for newer practitioners to address as they develop their own careers. One of the roles for experienced practitioners is to foster these important deliberative spaces to provide lifeblood for the future survival of the field.

Professionalism

One of the emerging themes from practitioner accounts is the way in which they created a new branch of postsecondary education practice – that is, distance learning practitioners. As Maggie Coats argued, it is about being 'professional in a profession', about having self-accountability. What does it mean to be a professional? The term professional is widely contested and as Furlong *et al.* (2000: 5) note, the wide field of education is fast-changing and complex.

> It is because professionals face complex and unpredictable situations that they need a specialised body of knowledge. If they are to apply that knowledge, it is argued that they need the autonomy to make their own judgements. Given that they have autonomy, it is essential that they act with responsibility – collectively they need to develop appropriate professional values.

Robson (2005) further develops these three constituents of professionalism: autonomy, professional knowledge and responsibility, and it is the notion of autonomy that I find enables us to consider individual agency. Yet as this book shows, professionals can be at loggerheads with attempts by managers within institutions to control them, as the very definition of 'professional' implies a degree of self-controlled autonomy within a community of practice, which is wider than any one institution. Lave and Wenger (1991: 115) define such a community as 'A set of relations among persons, activity and world, over time and in relation with other tangential and overlapping communities of practice'.

I argue that distance learning has created an area of professional practice which is an example of a community of practice. Access to this community of practice is vital if newcomers are to learn from each other. How can newcomers learn unless the taken-for-granted, tacit understanding that more experienced practitioners have is made explicit? I believe that reflective practice is fundamental to making such practical wisdom gained from experience explicit and testable. Where is its place in a book about distance learning? As I have argued elsewhere (Hillier 2006), reflective practice is not merely thinking about 'how things went'. It has to seek for ways to make a difference. It has to make the familiar strange and help make the tacit, informal theories that we hold explicit, so that we can further test them. The accounts from experienced practitioners in Part 2 offer a number of insights that newer professionals can draw upon. The participants needed to find 'better answers in certain contexts' rather than finding the right answer for all contexts. They are active in this pursuit, rather than waiting for ideas to come to them by sitting at their desks. Being reflective is not simply to understand the history of the field but to be able to test out the ideas that were developed in the early stages that have influenced practices since. Particularly because these practices were built on new ground, with few rules to govern them, we need to ask now what works, what effect these practices have, and whether we can think and do things differently. A powerful factor in such reflective practice is the community to which professionals belong, in other words the community of practice, or more accurately, *communities* of practice. I do not believe that distance learning is one homogenous practice. Indeed, it is clear from the accounts in this book that people's institutions, national postsecondary systems and identities influence what they do and how they do it. This book helps us all understand that community of practice and begin to participate within it.

What advice do I have for newer practitioners? Firstly, make sure you seek out members of your community. Although more experienced practitioners know how important the sense of belonging is, they may no longer have the luxury of time to reach out and make contact. So seek your colleagues out. Secondly, remember that you possess agency and use it. Do not wait for things to happen or to be told to do things in set ways 'because this has always been done like that'. This means that, thirdly, I encourage you to experiment. We do not know the best way to do things and every time you try out something even slightly differently, you can learn from the consequences. Fourthly, tell people what you are doing so that you can share this practice. Finally, I have exhorted folk to do this in the spirit of reflective practice and firmly believe that such an approach is fundamental to our evolving professional practice:

> We can argue that it is not the fact that we can change the world through critical reflection, or indeed can guarantee that we will change our daily practice, but that we have a more developed view about what we do than before we began to think reflectively.
>
> (Hamilton and Hillier 2006: 21–2)

References

Furlong, J., Barton, L., Miles, S. and Whitty, G. (2000) *Teacher Education in Transition.* Buckingham: Open University Press.

Hajer, M. and Wagenaar, H. (eds) (2003) *Deliberative Policy Analysis: Understanding Government in the Network Society.* Cambridge: Cambridge University Press.

Hamilton, M. and Hillier, Y. (2006) *The Changing Face of Adult Literacy, Language and Numeracy: A Critical History.* Stoke on Trent: Trentham Books.

Hillier, Y. (2006) *Reflective Teaching in Further and Adult Education,* 2nd edn. London: Continuum.

Lave, J. and Wenger, E. (1991) *Situated Learning: Legitimate Peripheral Participation,* 2nd edn. Cambridge: Cambridge University Press.

Robson, J. (2005) *Teacher Professionalism in Further and Higher Education.* London: Routledge.

10

Critical minds for a change

Michael Grahame Moore

Reading the chapters by Liz has been a journey down a lane of my own career memory, meeting many reflections and insights to provide significant pointers for action in today's world and directions for the future. I enjoyed 'hearing' from many colleagues. One of the characteristics of the generation we celebrate here has been our collegiality and friendships, born, as Ian Mugridge said, from a need to 'huddle together for warmth'.

It is this global or international character that Liz Burge has so beautifully captured in this book, and she has successfully avoided forcing an impression that the participants were the first people to conceptualize or establish programmes of distance learning. In the USA, Canada, Australia, South Africa and elsewhere, programmes of distance education have existed at postsecondary level since the end of the nineteenth century. The UK Open University owes most of its significant features to what was learned during planning travels overseas, especially to Wisconsin, South Africa and Australia by Harold Wiltshire, Michael Young, Chris Christodoulou and other members of the first planning committee, as well as the contributions of Charles Wedemeyer during his period of working in England with Walter Perry (Wedemeyer 1982). The combining of correspondence with television to create the original 'university of the air' concept had also been tested in England, with projects under the direction of Brian Groombridge and Walter James at the University of Nottingham in the mid-1960s. I personally benefited from their programmes when I used them to teach economics courses in Kenya around 1965. Even research and scholarship have a pedigree predating the period covered by this book, though I certainly agree with Tony Dodds's observation that we had no refereed journal articles and very few books (a history of scholarship can be found in Moore 2007). So, no, the participants were not the first distance educators. They were the first community of distance educators that was a truly international community, a community of like minds and similar personalities. They were leaders in a global movement, leaders in 'globalization' before such a concept had been invented.

In what ways were these pioneers 'similar personalities'? Well, whatever other characteristics they might share, one thing is clear: they were all, in one way or another, misfits, that is, they were rebelling against the conventional goals and procedures of the postsecondary education system. From an early age, some were academic misfits – Roger, Colin, Uli and Brian are outspoken on this, for example. Others became misfits only after beginning conventional careers, then jumping the university walls to travel into the unexplored territory of distance education. Whether early or late, everyone developed a particular, and for its time, unconventional personal vision. As history has evolved, we know now that their visions were valid, and the world of education has in general come to share them, but the movement has been in exactly that direction – the world came to them. They stepped outside in the first place; they became the innovators. Many were invariably lone voices, but, in time, the crowd followed.

What was it then, that inspired these leaders to step outside the mainstream? For most I believe there is no single answer, for leaders are complex people, driven by combinations of motives. However, common to most was a sense of annoyance, or in some cases anger, about the barriers set up by educational institutions to almost everyone except the already privileged members of society, for example, in the United Kingdom, Australia, Canada, Malaysia, New Zealand or the USA. The assumed superiority of those who were comfortably sheltered inside conventional higher education added insult to injury, and drove the typical pioneer into enough determination to show publicly that ordinary folk were as capable of benefiting from advanced and lifelong learning as were the elite.

Personally, one memorable experience that drove me to distance education was when I took over as the university's adult education program organizer in the equatorial city of Kisumu in Kenya and watched a lecture on political philosophy given to a handful of western-suited civil servants in the local community centre. After a while I became aware of the crowd of women subsistence (and illiterate) farmers, in town for the market, who were pressing against the windows of this big and mostly empty hall, excitedly chattering and pointing at the educational event going on inside. For me this sight epitomized the elitism and exclusion that characterized higher education. My recognition helped change the direction of my life. It obtained validity a few years later, when I moved to the USA to work with Charles Wedemeyer, the father of our field, and found a picture on his wall of a Russian serf boy standing at the door of a classroom. Like the children and adults I knew in Africa, the boy was denied the benefits of education because of his poverty, the need to work and the dreadfully inefficient distribution of educational resources. 'This is who we are here to serve' was Wedemeyer's explanation of why he kept the picture. He used the picture's title, *Learning at the Back Door*, for the title of the book that outlined his vision of distance education (Wedemeyer 1986). Opening up the back door, was later beautifully and metaphorically illustrated in the film *Educating Rita*, beloved by all adult educators. In one scene, Rita, the hairdresser, newly enrolled in the Open

University, finds herself seated next to a young man on a bus, he garlanded in his college scarf and reading a textbook. Rita asks, 'Are you a student?' and in reply to his supercilious affirmative, Rita retorts – and it meant so much more to her to able to say this than it did to him – 'So'm I'.

Among all the motivations and visions of the first generation of distance educators this was, I think, the most common and the most significant – to enable a universal population to be able to say, if they wanted to, that they too were entitled to learn, and able to learn. 'A universal population', yet paradoxically it was that majority who, from the point of view of higher education, were outsiders. I never cease to wonder at the sense of identification, recognition and attraction I feel in the company of the adult learners who present themselves for distance education. I think it is because they and I are kindred spirits, sharing some of the same personality characteristics reflected in the innovators in our field. These characteristics include a readiness to make sacrifices – of time, effort and usually money – in pursuit of long-term goals, accompanied by an energy driving them to live lives that are themselves acts of creativity. I have seen this in a semi-literate African farmer who told me he wanted to learn how to research the history of his tribe (not using exactly that terminology), in a 92-year-old Open University student who, when I asked what he would do after graduating said, 'there are so many exciting things to do in life', as well as in my current students who have abandoned jobs and home comforts in order to undertake doctoral study. There is much talk nowadays about communities of learners; they are, however, communities of idiosyncratic, independently-thinking individuals; people who are individualists before belonging to a collective, and far from being in any way conceivable as a 'class'. Idiosyncratic, innovative, creative: these characteristics distinguish the pioneers we read about in this book and those who would succeed them. Distance education is not yet a comfortable environment promising success for those who prefer to run with the crowd, to 'play it safe', and who are unduly respectful of convention and tradition (and long may it remain so!).

I found very little in the interviews that was surprising, although there are many points that I endorse as being especially important for the 'less experienced' student or practitioner (the two are not mutually exclusive of course!). First, try to capture for yourself some of the sense of excitement, the challenge, and what is referred to as 'passion and commitment' that has characterized the field to this point, because the satisfaction that you will enjoy if you get hooked on this work will outweigh any possible salary rewards or institutional status. This field is fun! This is exciting! If you don't get it, and I say this as kindly as I can, get out.

Next, please do not feel that because the book refers to the success of those involved in 'breaking new ground' that the game is over. Look around at the barriers, not only geographic but systemic, that lock learners into dependent relations with professors and educational institutions. Look for your chance of contributing to the needed revolution. Can you see how so many institutions of postsecondary education have allowed the ends of the institution to become subordinate to the means? Let me illustrate. I recently asked a faculty meeting to consider appointing more adjunct (part-time) teachers in their programme, and a professor objected, not because such instructors would harm students (they wouldn't) but on the grounds that such a move 'means the death of the professoriate'. Now surely the employment of professors or other human resources is a means to an end, and that end is the education of students and society generally? And surely that end should determine allocation of the resources? I ask you to take up the challenge of putting the professoriate as well as all the other vested interests in their proper places: that they should survive only as long as they prove responsive and contributive to learning and learners.

This illustration points to the more general observation that the pioneers have been about institutional reform. Their work has been about changing the culture of higher education; about changing the views held about learning and learners. It has been about changing views of the roles and responsibilities of teachers; in particular about the relative authority, power and control of the teaching and learning process. It has been about enfranchising and liberating learners. How ironic (or has it simply been an unrehearsed but brilliant strategy on the part of the pioneers?) that the general public has interpreted the distance education revolution of higher education to be nothing more than a matter of using technology in teaching?

Technology, of course, as every pioneer agrees, is both important and unimportant. It is important because communication via technology is a *sine qua non* (a foundational component) of distance education. It is unimportant in that the kinds of change we have worked to bring about, in learning, teaching and institutional management and policy, cut across all technologies. Further, the knowledge about learning, teaching, management and policy acquired when one technology was dominant frequently proved to be relevant and significant when technology changed, a point made by the participants. All share the concern about not 'reinventing the wheel', both in practice as well as in research and theory, which seems to be a particular problem in our field at the present time as a large number of people become intrigued by possibilities of new technology without being aware of the precedents. As emphasized by participants, reading the literature of distance education brings into perspective many facts and concepts understood by those of us who have worked for a long time in the field. This literature constitutes the theory, and it includes a common vocabulary that allows us to discuss, analyse, criticize, and – most important – build upon the theory through research. I advise young researchers to think of theory as being like a map: it summarizes what is known about a place, and it shows where there are unexplored spaces. So the theory is the basis for new exploration – that is, research. People who go on journeys of discovery – that is, do research without a theory, often ask questions that have been answered already, or that are unanswerable. Because they don't understand the vocabulary, they are confused; and then by desperately inventing new terminology that is not grounded in theory they cause further confusion. Much of the collected and reported literature is not significant, while questions that do need to be researched are often overlooked simply because the researchers do not know what is already known. So my appeal to the less experienced in the field is to take time to acquire at least a reading knowledge of what has been learned about distance education before venturing too far as either practitioner or researcher. Avoid being seduced into giving excessive attention to any particular communications technology. The theory of teaching and learning precedes the latest technology, and will survive it too.

To this appeal I add a (small) surprise I had when reading the interviews. Not only were some pioneers admitting to not being well read in distance education theory, of which, as we have agreed, there is little, but they were also not well educated in general educational theory. On the subject of training, I have seen no more powerful statement than that made by Janet Jenkins (Commonwealth of Learning 1990: 57):

> I had no special training for distance education and I have been trying to analyze what I missed . . . I made plenty of mistakes which might have been avoided if I had received training but these were not serious and I got on reasonably well. Looking back, however, I can see a major shortcoming. I was working without a frame of reference. I had no concept of distance education, and without an organizing framework my work lacked a clear direction and was less effective than it could have been.

I still find it hard to comprehend how it can be permissible to practise in higher education without training or qualification in being an educator. I believe that everyone taking responsibility for the lives of others by teaching should have some study of such fields as educational philosophy, educational psychology, management and policy, history and comparative studies, curriculum and instructional theory. In this I concur with what I understand to be Louise Moran's opinion. This is obviously a complex political problem, for what university administrator or minister of education would dare demand knowledge about teaching from his or her university teachers? Perhaps, however, the younger generation, who I am asked to address here, might see that it is in their own best interests to be better informed about the fundamentals of the field in which they propose to work: teaching and learning. I hope so.

Related to the issue of conceptual confusion resulting from lack of knowledge about theory, is the problem of what I suspect is deliberate misrepresentation of distance education by educational reactionaries whose intention is to use new technology to shore up old teaching methods and organizations, which they then hope to pass off as distance education. Since most university teachers are comfortable with that old pedagogy and that organization, they are happy to deliver courses on the internet as long as these resemble as closely as possible what goes on in the classroom. This approach does not require significant changes in resource allocation or the role of the teacher, and is popular with professors and administrators for those reasons. But it is counterproductive in several major ways. First, it fails to take advantage of the potential for much higher quality presentation of information that is possible through greater use of audio and video technologies. Second, it fails to take advantage of the economies of scale that would allow much higher sums to be invested in each course – not only for more specialists in content and instructional design but resulting in much higher production values in text, audio and video – provided the course is offered to a significantly larger population of students. Third, it denies instructors the time to attend to individual learners, as they have to spend so much on presenting information instead of facilitating their interaction with pre-designed materials. Fourth, it continues the wasteful duplication of programmes across institutions and the fragmentation of national or state resources that has contributed to making traditional higher education so costly. What this all adds up to is that if academic conservatives succeed in establishing the idea that distance education is no more than using technology, the reform of teaching and learning and of resource allocation in the interests of opening access and ensuring greater equity is dangerously threatened. If this book raises awareness about this threat among practitioners and students who have recently entered the field then, if for no other reason, it will make an invaluable contribution. The message is: 'don't be co-opted!'

References

Commonwealth of Learning (1990) *Perspectives on Distance Education: Report of a Round Table on Training Distance Educators.* Vancouver, BC : Commonwealth of Learning.
Moore, M.G. (2007) *Handbook of Distance Education,* 2nd edn. Mahwah, NJ: Lawrence Erlbaum Associates.
Wedemeyer, C.A. (1982) The birth of the Open University, a postscript, *Teaching at a Distance,* 21: 21–7.
Wedemeyer, C.A. (1986) *Learning at the Back Door: Reflections on Non-traditional Education Across the Life-span.* Madison, WI: University of Wisconsin Press.

11

On chaos, connection and challenge

David Murphy

'How do you react to what you've read?' was the essence of Liz's request. The overarching message is that something transformative occurred in the 1960s and 1970s that began to change the postsecondary educational environment and led to the expansion of educational access and choice for millions of learners around the globe. And the people interviewed for this book were an integral part of that critical period; indeed they helped shape it.

Coping with chaos

Certain phrases shine through and help us to capture the spirit of pioneering and creativity, such as 'no prior experience', 'we had to invent it' and 'on the edge'. In making sense of that quality of their experience, I was drawn back to two conceptual lenses I first used tentatively in a book chapter (Murphy and Taylor 1992) and then applied in my doctoral thesis (Murphy 1995) on instructional design: chaos theory and complexity theory. In the thesis, I relied heavily on the science of chaos to explain much of the work experience of instructional designers in distance education. Arguing that chaos theory, along with complexity theory, is the antithesis of traditional reductionist science, I made the point that chaos and complexity seek the fundamental rules that underlie complex systems, exposing the common concepts and self-organization that sustain them, and 'laying bare the fundamental mechanisms of nature' (Waldrop 1992: 39). The arguments developed relied on a picture of instructional design in distance education that was based on an open rather than a closed systems environment, a focus on complexity rather than simplicity, the need for a science of becoming rather than a science of being, and a recognition of irreversibility.

Chaos theory is the popular name used to describe 'the exploration of patterns emerging from apparently random events within a physical or social system' (Griffiths *et al.* 1991: 432). The term was 'playfully introduced into mathematics in 1968 (and earlier in the nineteenth century by Ludwig

Boltzmann in the context of thermodynamics)' (Knoespel 1991: 105). It is, in fact, seldom used by theorists and researchers in the physical sciences, where the designation is more usually dynamical systems methods or non-linear dynamics. At a basic level, the theory claims that, even within ostensibly stable systems (such as a swinging pendulum), chaotic behaviour can be observed, and within systems that seem chaotic, order can arise. You may know some of the more popular terms used in the theory, especially the 'butterfly effect', fractals, or the catchy phrase 'strange attractors'.

Chaos pursues the science of explanation rather than the science of prediction. Prediction is included, but only in the sense of knowing what kinds of systems, under what conditions, lead to evolutionary growth and creativity. It is thus not like aspects of physics, wherein trajectories can be predicted with high precision, but more like the sciences of geology and astronomy. In geology, for example, it does not seem possible to accurately predict earthquakes, but the conditions which lead to them and the processes which take place when they occur are well explained by geological theory and practice. It was with this sense of prediction that I offered my modelling of instructional design.

My thesis examined some of the issues and provided examples that affect the successful design and development of distance education courses. In particular, I focused on the role played by the instructional designer in the process, in an effort to discover what general approaches to the design task are effective. Evidence was offered that effectiveness is not necessarily achieved by striving for order. In fact, quite the opposite: during key periods of course development, a lack of imposed order leads to creative outcomes. The introduction of uncertainty and turbulence does, in some cases and under some conditions, move the instructional design system and outputs to a higher level.

The image that I offered from chaos theory was that of time-bound dissipative structures, interacting with their open environment at far-from-equilibrium conditions, and transforming themselves from disorder to order through bifurcation. In complexity terms, the related key phrase is the 'edge of chaos', which 'brings forth images of being poised in space, tentative, dangerous even, yet full of potential. Like all powerful phrases, the edge of chaos has stuck, and has become iconic for the immanent creativity of complex systems' (Lewin 1993: 53–4).

The point of my reiterating these principles lies in the potential parallels that emerge with respect to the explosive growth of distance education as a worldwide educational system. Can that growth be analysed and explained in terms of chaos and complexity theory? It is highly tempting, fuelled by the evocative statements made by Toffler (1984: xv) in the preface of Prigogine and Stengers' *Order Out of Chaos*:

> Most phenomena of interest to us are . . . *open* systems, exchanging energy or matter (and, one might add, information) with their environment. Surely biological and social systems are open, which means that

the attempt to understand them in mechanistic terms is doomed to failure.

This suggests, moreover, that most of reality, instead of being orderly, stable, and equilibrial, is seething and bubbling with change, disorder, and process ... At times, a single fluctuation or a combination of them may become so powerful, as a result of positive feedback, that it shatters the preexisting organization. At this revolutionary moment – the authors call it a 'singular moment' or a 'bifurcation point' – it is inherently impossible to determine in advance which direction change will take: whether the system will disintegrate into 'chaos' or leap to a new, more differentiated, higher level of 'order' or organization, which they call a 'dissipative structure.' (Such physical or chemical structures are termed dissipative because, compared with the simpler structures they replace, they require more energy to sustain them.)

Chapters 2 to 6 in this book reflect a system of postsecondary education undergoing rapid change and also some processes that led to a higher level of operation and effectiveness (along with an increase in energy required to sustain the system!). In reading the accounts from the participants, carrying their sense of profound purpose but at the same time challenged by uncertainty, newcomers may appreciate the worldwide upsurge in interest and application of distance education that formed the basis of a global phenomenon. Who would have predicted the massive growth and the emergence of the mega-universities? More pointedly in terms of chaos theory, was the UK Open University the 'fluctuation' that shattered the old ways and produced a new dissipative structure? Even more speculatively, has there been another more recent teetering on the creative edge of chaos that has faltered and led to turbulence and disorder? Here I refer to the demise of the UK e-university and other chaotic (and expensive!) ventures. Was there a previous bifurcation around 150 years ago with the emergence of correspondence education? What will the next bifurcation be?

At the heart of the argument is my point that reflective systems, or learning institutions, are the ones that seem most likely to or can move to the edge of chaos from either 'frozen' equilibrium or chaotic turbulence, and there maintain themselves to flourish and evolve. I invite you to think about your own institution and its relationship to any recent changes in postsecondary education. For myself (as I'm sure it is with many others), there is a sense that our institutions are becoming impossibly complex. At the same time, somehow we manage to work together, almost by accident at times, and order emerges (at times surprisingly!) from the chaos. Along these lines, if the conceptual lens here presented appeals to you, you might like to follow up on more recent literature on the links between chaos and education. A good starting point is *Complicity: An International Journal of Complexity and Education*, wherein you could try Gilstrap (2005).

The students

My other strong reaction in reading the chapters is 'It's the students!' I respond strongly to the vignettes, even the brief ones, when the interviewees mention specific students to illustrate certain points or to drive home their conviction that what they were doing felt so right at the time. Raj Dhanarajan's example of the wheelchair-bound graduating student whose child called out so compellingly, Ronnie Carr's instance of the cleaner who went eagerly to evening lectures and Patrick Guiton's long-distance visit to the multi-tasking bush student are all powerful illustrations of what may happen when educators calibrate their work in order to meet adult learners on their territory and in their mental spaces. The learners remain in our minds as affirmation that distance education has achieved significant results in some of the lives of the individuals it has touched.

Not surprisingly, this resonance made me reflect on the individual students who stood out in my mind over the past three decades. I want to mention three in particular. As you read you will realize that they stay in my mind for very different reasons. The first was a 17-year-old girl who had undergone shocking burns. As she embarked on a long journey of recovery, her therapists considered it would be helpful for her to continue her studies, and I was asked to help with mathematics. Although it was through 'external studies', my workplace was only a block or so from the hospital, so I began weekly visits that went on for 18 months or so. In that time I don't think she actually made great progress with the maths, but her progress through the treatment, operations, setbacks and growth is what stays with me. And it was a high point of a trip to visit remote students a couple of years later when my wife and I saw her at her rural home, looking immensely better than when I first met her, and heard her talk about going to work in rehabilitation.

At around the same time, I had a student who was a prison inmate. He was also studying maths, and made steady progress through one level and up to the next. As the examination drew nearer, arrangements were made for me to visit him in prison to assist with final revision. I had worked in the prison a few years' earlier, so was not concerned about the visit, though I had not been to the high security area where he was incarcerated. It was a sombre, sobering place, made all the more so by the demeanour of my student. He was rather disconnected, and his eyes seemed to dart in all directions, seldom looking straight at me. I remember asking him why he was studying maths, whether it was something he particularly enjoyed, and his reply was that they (the prison authorities) wouldn't let him study anything that included practical work. As I left, I talked with the staff about him, and as they explained his background, I slowly and chillingly realized that he was the person who a few years before had sadistically and brutally murdered someone I knew. I handed him over to another staff member.

Moving forward nearly two decades, and in an infinitely more positive vein, while in Hong Kong I worked on a great project with David Kember and others titled 'A Week in the Life of a Hong Kong Student'. The research involved students in most universities in Hong Kong, and the part of the particular investigation with which I was involved concentrated on distance education students at the Open University of Hong Kong. Rather boldly, we attempted a diary-interview approach and, to our delight, it worked. Enough students managed to maintain their diaries for a full week, and we were able to follow up with some fascinating interviews that teased out the details. Of our distance learners, there was one in particular who stood out, in terms of her self-discipline, perseverance and sheer hard work. Kar Ling was a nursing student, working full-time and balancing her study and home commitments with amazing self-organization and (mostly!) good humour. Our summary of a typical day follows:

> The weekend is not a time for rest and relaxation, as the first entry for Saturday clearly shows.
>
> > I get up at 05:20, and go to the hospital by bus at 05:30. I arrive at the hospital at 06:40 and go to work at 07:00. Then I have my breakfast with my colleagues. (Diary entry, Saturday)
>
> There is then the usual morning of work in the ward; joining the doctor for the ward round of prescribing treatment, giving instructions to the student nurses, preparing the injection chart, giving intravenous injections, checking treatment, monitoring intake and output charts, answering patients' questions and telephone queries, writing the nursing report, tracing an FNA (fine needle aspiration) report and collecting a swab culture from the laboratory. The lunch hour at noon is a welcome break, and allows her time to chat with her colleagues in the lunch room.
>
> In the two hours of work after lunch, Kar Ling treats a post-operational patient, admits a new patient and tends a patient with high fever. There are also administrative duties to fulfil, including the operation list for Monday.
>
> Leaving the ward at 3 pm, there is time for a quick bath before heading off by train to a tutorial. The tutorial runs for two hours from 4 pm, and Kar Ling contributes by answering some of the tutor's questions. There's time for some brief discussions with her classmates after the tutorial before heading for home.
>
> > I go home at 6:25 pm by KCR [train] and bus. Sleeping or thinking in the bus—thinking of the assignment. (Diary entry, Saturday)
>
> Although a welcome part of her study arrangements, the interaction that she has with both tutors and her fellow students can be frustratingly fleeting, or even unhelpful.
>
> > I also have no time to prepare for tutorials. I forget the data for tutorials since I have finished the suggested reading long time ago.

Sometimes, the data is new to me and I have not prepared for it. Thus, I do not understand.

It's nearly quarter to eight by the time Leung Kar Ling arrives home, where she enjoys dinner, followed by relaxing in front of the television and reading the paper. After an hour's rest at 9 pm, she gets back to some reading and preparing for the assignment before bed.

Despite her shift work, long travel times (yes, they can be time-consuming in Hong Kong) and the care of her two children (including helping the PTA and taking part in school activities), she managed 28 hours of study during the week. The research team eventually put together a book that told of the outcomes of the research, and a colleague and I penned a couple of chapters, one with the results and discussion in general and the other as a case study of this student. We published an amalgam of the two chapters in *Distance Education* (Murphy and Yum 1998), including a glimpse of this remarkable student.

So just as we as teachers remember our most inspirational (and most challenging) students, so as students we recall our most inspirational (and our worst!) teachers. Not surprisingly, this awareness tends to influence my practice today. I vividly recall Professor Kockendorfer in Pure Maths 1, the only university lecturer I experienced who received sustained and enthusiastic applause from his large lecture hall of usually somewhat disinterested students. Despite his difficulties with English (having recently escaped from East Germany – this was 1969), his sheer enthusiasm and joy in the 'discovery' of mathematics that he shared with us laid the seeds for some of my later teaching the same subject at a distance. My experience with distance mode students also enhances my motivation to do the utmost to support them by creating the highest quality teaching and learning environments that our staff can manage. The need for such motivation and quality of professional work is echoed by the interviewees in this book. I wonder, though, about today's contexts: what conditions now are prompting such motivation and quality?

On knowing and connecting

In perusing the chapters, I reacted to the advice given about 'being knowledgeable', particularly the comments about getting to know the literature and not assuming that anything more than five years old is not worth reading. It reminded me that the Open University (UK) journal *Teaching at a Distance*, the precursor to *Open Learning* (which began in 1986) contains real gems for today's practitioners and researchers, not to mention some intriguing and catchy titles – how could I ever forget 'The Case for Coarser Courses'? My point is that such a useful resource should be made more available. I cannot be the first to suggest that they be scanned and digitized for the web. And there are all those early issues of *Distance Education* (originating from Australia in 1980), *Journal of Distance Education* (from Canada in 1986) and *The American Journal of Distance Education* (from the USA in 1987). Do you know the author and title of the first article in each first issue? If you do, it probably betrays your age or decades of experience in the field. If you are regularly scanning the contents pages of their current issues, at least you are well connected intellectually to what is occurring.

In Chapter 2, 'Facing challenges', the subheading 'No prior experience' brought back further memories from decades ago. I became involved in distance education by accident rather than design, in about 1974. As a result of some administrative errors and lack of communication regarding a job application, I ended up in what was then called an 'External Studies' department of the Hobart College of Technical and Further Education (TAFE) responsible for teaching mathematics. I faced the semester due to start the next week, students enrolled in the three subjects I would care for, and no materials prepared! I cringe as I recall the quality (or lack of same) of the study guides I prepared to accompany the textbooks. I wonder if any young staffers have similar experiences today, and with what consequences?

And while on the subject of quality, I will add a word of advice on contributions to its achievement. Yes, by all means become a reflective practitioner, and apply whatever version of the quality cycle to which your institution adheres. But beyond this activity, learn to work as a member of a team. I strongly argue that the best work I have done over the decades (especially in course development) has been as a result of belonging to an effective team. This strategy is nothing new: the course team approach has underpinned institutions like the Open University (UK) throughout its history, and receives attention (albeit rather briefly!) in this book. I also believe that this teamwork has kept me in good standing and firmly attached to my basic principles as I have worked in more mainstream postsecondary contexts, such as my first stint in academic staff development, where the success of a number of 'flexible learning' initiatives was contingent on effective teamwork. How far such teamwork is feasible today in postsecondary institutions is a question for you to think about.

Overall, reflecting on the fascinating material revealed in this book, alongside my own experience of postsecondary teaching in both face-to-face and at a distance modes, my conclusion is that my distance education activity has been the more challenging and rewarding. And that is my key message – it's more rewarding *because* it's more challenging. This near-paradox has been the experience of our interviewees – the pioneers who led the way, took chances and showed us just what is possible through distance education.

References

Gilstrap, D.L. (2005) Strange attractors and human interaction: leading complex organizations through the use of metaphors, *Complicity*, 2(1): 55–70, online at http://www.complexityandeducation.ualberta.ca/COMPLICITY2/ Complicity2_TOC.htm.

Griffiths, D.E., Hart, A.W. and Blair, B.G. (1991) Still another approach to adminis-tration: chaos theory, *Educational Administration Quarterly*, 27(3): 430–51.

Knoespel, K.J. (1991) The emplotment of chaos: instability and narrative order, in N.K. Hayles (ed.) *Chaos and Order: Complex Dynamics in Literature and Science.* Chicago: University of Chicago Press.

Lewin, R. (1993) *Complexity: Life on the Edge of Chaos.* London: J.M. Dent.

Murphy, D. (1995) Chaos rules: an exploration of the work of instructional designers in distance education. Doctoral thesis, Deakin University.

Murphy, D. and Taylor, G. (1992) A tale from the mud, in M.S. Parer (ed.) *Developing Open Learning Courses.* Churchill, Australia: Monash Distance Education Centre.

Murphy, D. and Yum, J. (1998) Understanding Hong Kong distance learners, *Distance Education*, 19(1): 64–80.

Toffler, A. (1984) Science and change, in I. Prigogine and I. Stengers, *Order Out of Chaos: Man's New Dialogue with Nature.* New York: Bantam Books.

Waldrop, M.M. (1992) *Complexity: The Emerging Science at the Edge of Order and Chaos.* New York: Simon & Schuster.

12

Resilience, relevance and realism

Diana G. Oblinger

Purpose. You heard it in all the interviews of our distance learning pioneers. They all possess a strong sense of purpose. It is a good place to begin. Although we all rush through life with too many meetings to attend, emails to respond to and tasks to complete, it is important to pause periodically to consider the underlying purpose of higher education. Otherwise, how can we be sure of our direction?

The purpose of higher education

Society has expectations of what it should receive in return for the trust, personal investment and public money that are invested in higher education. There are three public purposes for higher education.

One goal is workforce preparation. However, simply being prepared for a job is not enough. Workforce preparation implies being ready for whatever job, career or challenge comes your way. It is a skill set – and a mindset – that involves continuous learning. Another goal of postsecondary education is social mobility. College prepares learners for better paying jobs as well as for more active participation in society. Distance education has significantly advanced both workforce preparation and social mobility. But the third goal, developing an educated citizenry, is critical as well. The ability (and responsibility) to understand issues and make informed decisions undergird a democracy. Without an educated and engaged citizenry, our societies will flounder.

The conclusion is obvious: education is a social imperative. To a great degree, personal and professional success depends on an excellent education. And social well-being is tied to a well-educated populace. The belief in this social imperative lies behind the motivation of many – if not all – of our distance learning pioneers. It is an imperative none of us should forget.

Listening to learners

The pioneers spoke repeatedly about serving learners and listening to learners. It is a trait we should all strive to embody. If our programmes are not relevant to learners' needs, we do everyone a disservice.

Of course, one of the great challenges today is that we are educating more people than ever before. Their characteristics, preparation, motivation and learning styles are incredibly diverse. And they need support, not just with learning, but in the other activities that impact on their success – financial support, technology access, career selection, and so on.

Many of today's students favour different learning styles than my generation's learning style. For example, their learning preferences tend toward group study, experiential activities, the use of technology and engagement. This generation learns by doing – sometimes doing multiple activities at once. We mustn't assume they are like us.

All too often we make assumptions about who our learners are or what they value only to find out that we were wrong. This may be painfully true with our younger learners. For example, we observe students using technology without fear and assume that means they understand the technology. For a great many, that is not true. Texting on a mobile phone or having a profile in Facebook doesn't mean a learner knows how to use PowerPoint or Excel. And, although search engines provide information when queried, the results are not necessarily all of high quality. Students may naïvely assume that there is no real difference. We also presume that their constant connection to the web means they want to learn via the web. Not always true. Listening to learners is a very active process – one that is much more than listening to our own well-intended assumptions.

Listening is critical when it comes to defining success, as well. Although our definition of success might be receiving a diploma, success to a distant learner might be different. As our pioneers illustrated, we must listen to be sure we aren't imposing our definitions on others. Gaining enough skill to advance to the next pay grade or returning to school after retirement to learn for the joy of it may constitute success to a learner. As our pioneers said: context matters – the context of the learner.

Teams

A lesson we have all learned is that people are more likely to be successful when they work as a team. No one person has all the skills that are needed to bring together a robust learning environment. Distance education is more than an assembly of individual courses. In fact, we must continue to challenge ourselves to move beyond the notion of a course as covering content, to constructing a series of learning and support environments. Effective learning doesn't just convey content, but motivates the learner, develops skills and enables them to transfer their newly-learned skills to other settings. Interaction is a critical part of the learning experience. Assembling the pedagogical, technical, managerial and financial skills is facilitated thorough common goals, clear communication and strong project management. It may require reorganization, new responsibilities and retraining.

Teams are also important for the diversity of perspective they bring. Debate and dialogue help us see options and wrestle with choices. And, as some of the pioneers observed, including students on the team is helpful. After all, who better understands the learner's perspective than the learner?

Unlearning

To make the future, we must sometimes 'unlearn' the past. This means giving up mental models that may no longer be effective, such as letting go of the notion of learning as assimilation and instead thinking of active learning. Our pioneers challenged many assumptions, such as online learning being lower in quality than face-to-face learning. Other assumptions, such as assuming online communication *replaces* face-to-face communication, must be challenged. One mode of communication doesn't cancel the other; they coexist.

The challenges of distance education aren't over. Although we've had many successes, the environment continues to change. Learners, our notions of what it means to be educated, the technologies we have at our disposal and the stakes of success (or failure) create turbulence. The only dependable advantage in turbulent times is the ability to reinvent ourselves before circumstances force us to – a characteristic called resiliency: 'Strategic resilience is not about responding to a one-time crisis. It's not about rebounding from a setback. It's about continuously anticipating and adjusting ... It's about having the capacity to change before the case for change becomes desperately obvious' (Hamel and Valikangas 2003: 55). Those who follow our pioneers cannot rest on their laurels.

Future challenges

Our pioneers were relentless realists, dealing with the world as it was rather than how they wished it might be. That is a lesson we all might learn: 'The future is less unknowable than it is unthinkable, less inscrutable than unpalatable' (Hamel and Valikangas 2003: 55).

The need for distance education will continue, but predicting the future based on the past may not be helpful, just as our pioneers observed. To be resilient, organizations must 'dramatically reduce the time it takes to go from "that can't be true" to "we must face the world as it is" ' (Hamel and Valikangas 2003: 56). If we look at our current environment, many of our challenges will come from the emerging digital culture. Some call this emerging culture web 2.0. It goes beyond email and basic websites, to social networking, augmented reality and wikis. Web 2.0 is all about interacting with information and with people. Information flows in multiple directions, is user-generated and is shared widely. Participation becomes as important as consumption (Lorenzo *et al.* 2006). A few features may be particularly relevant to the future of distance education: they are choice, co-creation, distributed cognition, distributed learning communities and multi-modal contexts.

Choice

Due to proliferation of information on the internet, as well as tools that allow individualization, choice has become an expectation. Tivo made it possible to choose what you want to watch on TV and when. MP3 players made it possible for users to select their music and construct individualized playlists with audio that can be accessed any time and anywhere. The choices are almost infinite. Mobile phones can access the internet, take photos, provide geolocation information and more. We are surrounded by – and expect – choices. Is this same level of choice reflected in our current distance learning environments? Should it be in the future?

Co-creation and participation

Beyond a tool to connect people, the web has become a medium for participation. Users are not limited to receiving information – they can comment, collaborate and create their own content. Wikipedia exemplifies the growing number of tools that enable co-creation and participation. Anyone can create and publish her or his own content. But that content no longer stands alone: commentary, sharing, and debate allow anyone interested to participate (Lorenzo *et al.* 2006).

For example, blogging has emerged as a participatory medium. It has changed journalism. Major media organizations are not the only ones who can comment on trends, file reports or provide editorials. Anyone who wants to share an opinion can. Sites such as Digg.com make it easy to share opinions and rank the top stories of the week. And wikis and collaborative editing tools allow for the co-creation of documents. Is this same level of participation and co-creation reflected in our current distance learning environments? Should it be in the future?

Distributed cognition

A significant shift was signalled by the emergence of Wikipedia: distributed cognition. The collective intelligence of many can be marshalled, irrespective of time or place. Rather than expertise being reserved for designated experts, it can exist among amateurs. Those amateurs, through collaboration, revision and co-creation can assemble useful, accessible bodies of knowledge. It also signals a significant shift in the locus of control. 'Experts' are not just those who possess specific credentials; 'experts' are those who, for the love of the subject, work to advance the art and science of the field. Is distributed cognition reflected in our current distance learning environments? Should it be in the future?

Distributed learning communities

Although distributed learning was once synonymous with distance learning, it has taken on new meaning in a web 2.0 world. Powerful pedagogical models go well beyond what was possible in a traditional classroom by providing opportunities for guided enquiry with active knowledge construction. Students don't just learn about science, for example, they *do* science. But what they work on need not be physically located with them. Through remote instruments and the emerging cyberinfrastructure, students can participate in activities without being physically present. Students can apprentice with senior scientists and be mentored because virtual communities allow individuals from a variety of locations to come together. Learning is distributed across the classroom, home, work and the community. And the digital environment allows functions to be distributed among individuals as well as tools (e.g. graphing, visualization, animation) (Dede 2006). Are distributed learning communities a fundamental part of our current distance learning environments? Should they be?

Multi-modal contexts

In a world where text, images, video, audio and geolocation are all potential forms of communication, few 'conversations' are homogeneous; an increasing number are multi-modal. Similarly, the most effective learning environments may be multi-modal, integrating videoconferencing, asynchronous threaded discussions, synchronous virtual interactions (e.g. meetings in the virtual world, Second Life) networking, small group collaboration using groupware or face-to-face interaction. The environments facilitate different activities (e.g. brainstorming, social interaction, developing new conceptual frameworks, etc.) and may build on the strengths (or weaknesses) of individual students (Dede 2006). Are our current distance learning environments multi-modal? Should they be?

Lessons learned

As I reflect on our distance education pioneers and think about the future, there are six lessons I will carry with me:

- *Monitor your environment and be ruthlessly realistic.* It is important to be in touch with users, understand the technological environment and be sensitive to the local social conditions if education is to be successful. This implies not seeing the world as we might like, but as it really is. We must be ruthless with ourselves, never just assuming that we know but being sure we have done the investigations that guarantee that we know.
- *Understand the goals and your audience.* Education is designed to serve people. If we are to serve learners, we must understand them as well as their goals. If an individual's goal is to move from a labour position to a desk job, then a Ph.D. programme is inappropriate for that learner. Rather than assuming our goals and preferences hold true for all, we must understand those we wish to serve.
- *Be creative.* For many of the challenges education will face, today's solutions won't suffice. We need to challenge our assumptions, look beyond comfortable examples and try new things.
- *Measure and revise.* However, just because we have conceptualized a unique solution doesn't mean that it is effective. Do we routinely collect feedback from users? Do we measure the effectiveness of our programmes? Do we compare our results to those of others? Because so much is at stake for our learners we must measure our results and revise our processes. The spirit of continuous improvement should be part of our *modus operandi.*
- *Work as a team.* Providing education and ensuring learners are successful is a complex endeavour. No single person – or unit – can do it alone. Teams have goals in common. They share information and support each other – intellectually and emotionally – because the ultimate outcome is worth working for.
- *Be resilient.* The goals of education remain constant, but the world around us will continue to change – perhaps at an ever-increasing rate. Rather than becoming rigid in our organizations, processes and mindsets we must try to be flexible and adaptable.

As Alvin Toffler observed, the illiterate of the twenty-first century will not be those who cannot read and write, but those who cannot learn, unlearn and relearn. We have been privileged to learn from these distance learning pioneers. But we cannot stop there. We must continue to unlearn and relearn, because ensuring education is available to all is an imperative.

References

Dede, C. (2006) Teaching and learning with cyberinfrastructure, EDUCAUSE Learning Initiative web seminar presentation, 7 November 2006, www.educause.edu/ELIWEB0611.

Hamel, G. and Valikangas, L. (2003) The quest for resilience, *Harvard Business Review*, 81(9): 52–63.

Lorenzo, G., Oblinger, D. and Dziuban, C. (2006) How choice, co-creation, and culture are changing what it means to be Net savvy, EDUCAUSE Learning Initiative Paper no. 4, www.educause.edu/ir/library/pdf/ELI3008.pdf.

13

Culture, technology, and making choices

Barbara Spronk

When I was approached to be a commentator on the findings from this project, I was only too happy to accept. Now, however, having seen the richness of these findings, I find myself overcome by the humility that many of the distance educators interviewed here are urging on their colleagues new and old. I am definitely in the 'old' category, having lived with distance education as my constant companion, on a number of continents, for over three decades. What can I possibly add to their wisdom, experience and advice? Not much, apart from a few observations of a 'framing' nature, to do with cultural diversity, the newest technologies, and the ideological and political frameworks that support them. Then, in conclusion, rather than offer advice or suggestions to my fellow distance educators, I enter a plea that we continue to work towards the formative ideals of which our interviewees have spoken so powerfully.

Observation one: the challenges of cultural diversity

First, what struck me in reading these chapters was hearing the voices of many long-time friends and colleagues, calling up memories of many spirited discussions centred on 'What are we trying to do here, and what are we *really* doing?' At base, all of us were trying to provide learners with the most effective learning experiences available under the circumstances. Those circumstances involved geographical distances, between learner and providing institution, learner and teacher, learner and learner. Those we could overcome, with varying success, by means of technological links. To deal with other kinds of distance, such as the cognitive distance between a learner who had never finished school and an academically demanding set of materials and learning tasks, we worked to design materials that would engage the learner where she or he was, and provided as many kinds of support for that learner that we could afford – tutors, advisers, counselors, library services, technical support, and user-friendly administrative systems run by trained and attentive staff.

Cultural distances, however, were and are much more intractable, partly because they are less talked about, and mostly because they are less well understood, if at all. There are practical considerations as well. Learner-centredness takes us only so far; in the end we have to produce a set of materials and ways of supporting and facilitating the learning that is supposed to happen based on those materials that would meet most learners' needs. We do not know nearly enough about those learners and their needs. Who has the time, the tools, the knowledge or the budget to do the needed analyses? And if we actually did the analyses, what would we be able to do, realistically, with the results? We are seldom able to customize courses to individual circumstances (Empire State College's 'learning contract' model is a significant exception to this statement), because of budget constraints, institutional dynamics and political pressures, and the numbers of learners for whom we must make provision.

Cultural distance confronts all distance educators. Distance educators, especially in the so-called settler countries of Canada, the USA, Australia and New Zealand, have been continually challenged by the need to take cultural diversity into account in developing and delivering courses and programmes, even though these challenges have received only occasional attention in the literature. The populations of these settler countries are by definition culturally diverse, having been the product originally of colonization and subsequently of continuing waves of immigration; the countries of the European Union are also coping with an increasingly diverse range of peoples, thanks to immigration and transnational integration policies. Official bi- or trilingualism and multiculturalism, in countries such as Canada, Belgium and Switzerland, present further challenges. As a consequence, mainstream programmes offered by distance means may involve a sizeable minority of learners whose first language is something other than the language in which the materials are written, and whose culture is not reflected accurately or adequately in the learning materials. This is doubly or triply so for the first, internally colonized, peoples of these regions – Canada's First Nations, the native peoples of the USA, Australia's Aboriginal peoples, the Maori of New Zealand. Distance education, and especially open education, programmes have been important educational and empowerment vehicles at both secondary and postsecondary levels for these learners, many of whom live in Third World conditions in some of the most affluent countries on earth.

In the world's poverty zones, potential learner populations for distance education programmes are even more diverse. On the continents of Africa, Asia and South America, the agents of conquest and colonization grouped and divided peoples according to political and administrative expediency. The consequence is a set of nation states in which the languages spoken number in the dozens or even hundreds and where racial, ethnic and religious affinities and divisions provide the raw material on which are enacted multiple and sometimes bloody struggles of identity and resistance. This diversity receives little attention in the distance education literature. The narratives or analyses that do emerge from distance education practice in these contested states tell of the challenges of lack of resources, infrastructure and trained personnel, but seldom of the nearly impossible task of meeting the needs of such diverse populations. We need to hear more. Fortunately, we are beginning to hear more, thanks to the fact that the literature of distance education is less and less the monopoly of associations, institutions and publishers in affluent countries. The Commonwealth of Learning is doing a great deal to make available the experiences and knowledge of those who are coping directly with these issues in the countries of South Asia, sub-Saharan Africa, the Caribbean and the Pacific. The Association of Asian Open Universities makes its conference proceedings available in English. Distance education journals in countries such as India and Turkey are also published in English. The *Journal of Distance Education* publishes in both French and English. To a great extent, however, many of us whose first language is English are still held prisoner by our language, unable to take advantage of insights of distance educators who work and publish in other languages. That same limitation applies to the present volume: as valuable as the reflections of these distance education pioneers are, they are a subset of a much larger pool of wisdom and accumulated experience that resides in countries from whose distance educators we are still hearing, and learning, too little.

Observation two: the new technologies – here to stay?

This neglect of issues of cultural diversity in the distance education literature appears to be lessening somewhat, however, with the advent of online learning. Courses online are immediately available to learners anywhere in the world who have the resources required to access them. Distance education providers, both public and private, have been quick to seize the opportunity that online delivery provides for truly global reach to market their courses worldwide. Many of these offerings are at postgraduate level, in the field of distance education itself (witness the Masters of Distance Education programmes that are available online from Maryland and Oldenburg, the UK Open University, Athabasca University and the University of London/IEC) and in business subjects, particularly the MBA. These programmes are expensive, and learners – increasingly termed 'customers' or 'consumers' in the language of the education marketplace – are choosing among the programmes on offer with quality and value for money as prime considerations. Among the criteria these consumers are applying in their decisions are (1) relevance of content to their local situations; and (2) recognition in the service or support components of their geographical, political and cultural realities. Providers are in turn discovering that in order to provide satisfactory learning experiences to this international audience they must pay increased attention to matters of culture. Articles and books are now beginning to appear that deal with the culture of learners and the cultural and ethical implications of the internet as a vehicle for teaching and learning (e.g. Gayol and Schied undated; Lea and Nicoll 2002; Tait and Mills 2003).

Another of the big questions being asked about the presence of these new information and communication technologies in education, in addition to their cultural and ethical implications, is their likely longevity. Are they here to stay, or will they, as several of those interviewed for the preceding chapters suggest, go the way of all the other technologies that were going to work miracles in education? I have been around long enough to see a number of technologies wax and then wane in popularity, each of them heralded in the distance education literature as *the* technology that was going to revolutionize and transform teaching and learning. None of them has done so. And while none of them has disappeared from use, they have pretty much disappeared from the distance education literature.

That literature is now dominated by information and communication technologies. A few years ago, when this current obsession began to take hold, I was prepared to write off information and communication technologies as yet another craze. By this time I was working for the International Extension College, whose focus and mission centred on innovative approaches to education in the developing world. Computer-mediated communication seemed a distant dream for most of the organizations and institutions with which we were working, and I and my colleagues – all experienced distance educators – prepared ourselves to ride out yet another wave. Doubtless, we thought, this one would deposit us on the beach yet again, where we would wait for the next wave to come along.

Well, we are all still riding, and there is no beach in sight. I would like to suggest some reasons for what may be the staying power of these technologies, in terms of how this innovation differs from other recent innovations, and of the social and political forces that are promoting and supporting its use in education.

First, what makes information and communication technologies, and in particular the internet and the web so different from other technological innovations is the integrative power of the web. It is possible to convert virtually all forms of information, from text to photographs to feature-length movies, into digital format. Thanks to computer networking, once voice and graphic images are represented in digital format, they can be manipulated on a computer and/or transmitted on a computer network around the world almost instantly.

Never before has there been a technology that offers so much potential for integrating all manner of information, thereby changing dramatically the variety, amount, sources and media of information required for learning. Moreover, the potential of the communicative aspects of the technology to reduce significantly that old bogey of distance education – students' isolation from each other and from their tutors or instructors – makes this technology almost irresistible. Further securing the power of information technology in education is the support it receives from the process of globalization.

Observation three: ideological and historical choices

Educational innovations such as web-based education and flexible learning are not strictly technological developments, nor are they technologically determined. A host of ideological and historical choices are at work in education as in other spheres of life in the twenty-first century, including deficit-cutting and government downsizing, privatization, free trade and deregulation. All of these play a part in the larger restructuring process that has become popularly known as 'globalization'. Capitalism has become truly universalized. In this process, economic units are becoming uncoupled from the social constraints of local and national communities; assets are being transferred from the public sector to the private; and power is being consolidated into the hands of ever-larger corporate units that represent an ever-shrinking proportion of the world's population (e.g. Menzies 1996: 89).

The technological revolution is a material dynamic of globalization. Global-scale corporations, particularly in the information, financial and communication sectors, can exploit the global information network as a 'unified system' of production, marketing, distribution and consumption. In the ideological dimension, the corresponding dynamic of globalization is a neo-liberal development agenda that emphasizes the centrality of the market and market forces. Responding to the needs of capital in a now global context, the voices of power call for a less interventionist state in economic and social arenas, and propose measures that include deregulation, decentralization and privatization.

Both dynamics are operating in the arena of education, in complementary and connected ways. As I have written elsewhere (Spronk 2003), the neo-liberal agenda for education is being played out worldwide in terms of the following measures:

- Shift of public funding for education from higher to lower levels of education (e.g. the global drive to implement Universal Primary Education by 2015).
- Reduction of public spending on education at all levels, by increasing class size and teacher-student ratios, shifting costs to the user – now called a 'consumer' rather than a 'student' – and encouraging private enterprise initiatives intent on capturing the lucrative 'education market'.
- Expansion of secondary and higher education through increased privatization.
- The drive for 'comparative advantage' in terms of attracting investment, emphasizing the need for labour pools that are highly skilled, especially in

those tasks needed for the 'information/knowledge society', but at the same time low-waged.

• Regulatory systems that emphasize accountability, giving rise to managerial and business models in school and university governance and an emphasis on results measured by standard tests at all grade levels.

• Uniform standards with instrumental ends, geared to producing graduates with the skills required by a 'high-tech' labour market (e.g. the 'back to the basics' movement in schools that emphasizes maths, sciences and language over literature and the arts).

• Looking to the information and communication technologies that are being produced by multinational companies and used to such powerful effect by finance capital, to work their magic in educational institutions at all levels, in tasks that include delivery of cost-effective programming, facilitation of international and multi-level collaborations and creation of administrative efficiencies.

Information technologies in education fulfil admirably various features of this agenda. Here are a few examples, which reinforce comments made by several of the interviewees:

• Costs of equipment, software and connectivity are shifted to the user, especially in the case of learners who are studying at a distance from an institution, whether by choice or circumstance; frequently costs of printing are also offloaded onto users, who have the option of learning entirely online, or printing off what they wish to read in hard copy, at their own expense.

• Private educational enterprises, such as the University of Phoenix, can set up shop 'globally' with little investment in physical plant, by hiring part-time instructors, off-campus or even offshore who, using their own equipment and internet accounts, develop and deliver online courses to anyone anywhere, typically in market-demand areas such as business studies and 'high tech' computing.

• Public and private institutions, financed by private investors in anticipation of a profit, form consortia as vehicles for delivering ('showcasing') their courses worldwide via the web.

• Public institutions can also readily and at almost no extra cost (apart from copyright clearances) export their online courses to an international audience and bring in much-needed revenue to offset reductions in government funding.

• In terms of cost-cutting for institutions, corporate developers of hardware and software and their marketing agents will supply their products for use in educational settings at reduced prices – or in some cases as a corporate donation – as a way of getting students accustomed to using a particular product and influencing their eventual purchase decisions.

• Institutions use computer and telecommunications applications extensively to manage all aspects of their operations – finances, student records, inventories, course and examination scheduling, personnel files, satellite campuses, etc. – with greater efficiency, transparency and hence account-ability than was possible with paper-based systems.

- Teaching via the web is an appropriate way of equipping students to use the web and its associated technologies once they are in the labour force, making them more marketable 'products' of the institution. High rates of employment for graduates also serve to raise the institution's profile in the education marketplace.
- Institutions, whether public or private, at least in the affluent world, are increasingly under pressure to adopt information technologies for teach-ing and learning in order to attract students who have a multitude of choices in an education marketplace that, thanks to online delivery, is now truly global. Institutions that offer choice and flexibility in modes and media of learning are more appealing to sophisticated 'consumers'.

Conclusion: back to the future

For all these reasons, my inclination is to believe that in some form, these new technologies are here to stay in education. I also believe, however, that we must take seriously the choices we have in terms of using them. And we do have choices: there is no unstoppable imperative operating here, powerful though the prevailing economic and political agendas may be. For those of us still committed to the notion of education as a public good, education is not a privilege but rather a right that states and communities have a duty to protect. Open and distance education approaches in particular continue to offer powerful tools for providing access to educational opportunities, not just enhanced markets for educational goods. In order to use these tools for access and success, however, we must continue to ask ourselves the questions that the distance education pioneers asked and are still asking.

First, what are you trying to do?

- Open access to the multitudes, as is the task in so many developing coun-tries? Online learning as it is delivered now is not likely to meet your needs, since it is so demanding of staff and other resources. You may still be able to incorporate the resources of the web, or some administrative email, or wireless technologies (e.g. mobile telephone) into your delivery model, however, without the costs of full online delivery, in a blended model that uses a variety of technologies old and new.
- Serve the needs of a very specific and relatively affluent group? Online delivery could well be an excellent fit, depending on the skills and knowledge you are needing to impart.

Second, what are you really doing? This is where honesty is fundamental.

- Perhaps you are really trying to extend access to presently underserved or even marginal groups? If so, you need to ask yourself hard questions about the extent to which you are actually reaching those groups, and if you are not, what barriers, such as cost or access to required technologies, are getting in the way.

- Perhaps what you are really doing is finding ways to use the latest technologies. If so, you need to ask yourself why. Perhaps that is what funding agencies are demanding; perhaps all your competitors are using these technologies so you feel you must as well; perhaps you are simply enamoured of the machines and their promise. In all these cases, be aware of your priorities, in which learners' needs and pedagogies appropriate to meeting those needs may be far down the list.
- Perhaps you are really trying to make some money by adding a lot of students to your rolls by putting them online and using the cheapest labour available to provide academic support (sessionals, teaching assistants, volunteers). Your goal of making money is understandable in the face of shrinking funding. Be aware, however, of the old business adage that if your goal is to do something cheaply, quickly and effectively, you can have two out of three. Take your pick.
- Perhaps you are trying to achieve the ideal of providing as many people as possible with the best learning experiences that are available. That, I would argue, is what distance education is really all about, and by reading the foregoing chapters you probably have a substantial portion of the advice and guidance you will need. I commend you in your struggle; you are in good company!

References

Gayol, Y. and Schied, F. (undated) Cultural imperialism in the virtual classroom: critical pedagogy in transnational distance education, retrieved 15 January 2004, from www.geocities.com/Athens/Olympus/9260/culture.html.

Lea, M. and Nicoll, K. (eds) (2002) *Distributed Learning: Social and Cultural Approaches to Practice.* London: The Open University.

Menzies, H. (1996) *Whose Brave New World? The Information Highway and the New Economy.* Toronto: Between the Lines Press.

Spronk, B. (2003) Open classrooms and globalisation: connections and reflections, in J. Bradley (ed.) *The Open Classroom: Distance Learning in and out of Schools.* London: Kogan Page.

Tait, A. and Mills, R. (eds) (2003) *Rethinking Learner Support in Distance Education: Change and Continuity in an International Context.* London: Routledge Falmer.

Part 4

Assessing relevance

14

Continuing construction: where now?

Liz Burge

We have seen what it takes for 44 pioneers to 'break new ground' in postsecondary education; to set up new forms or 'constructions' of educational delivery. Being 'part of something quite extraordinary' (Roger Mills), the pioneers demolished or reduced many barriers to postsecondary education. Establishing new academic 'structures' and systems was, in effect, 'crafting the future' (Shona Butterfield) for them and their adult students. Being 'restless realists' (Diana Oblinger), refusing to fit into the values and methods of traditional postsecondary delivery (Michael Grahame Moore), or as Sir John Daniel put it, being unhappy with the 'old dispensation', they worked from the ground up, sometimes without very clear plans. They developed the skills to remain determined, exist on the edges of their knowledge, insist on overt quality standards, achieve learning outcomes comparable with classroom forms of delivery and endure public doubt or outright criticism. These usually fearless but never reckless pioneers built on the principles of respect and responsiveness, flexibility and assured quality. The resulting strategies recognized diversity in learners, client-centred learning services, context-sensitive decision-making and integration of technologies old and new. Sometimes the pioneers used strategic stealth – working beneath the levels of bureaucratic detection, especially when fledging innovations needed protection or support. Notably, they found much of their general activity 'exciting' – the most often used adjective to represent the key affective quality of their experience.

Reading about such pioneering experience is educational, but so what? Which aspects of their knowledge seem relevant for today's contexts? Where might the pioneers' constructions of knowledge be continued? What will encourage and inspire their successors? Yvonne Hillier reminded me that reflective practice is not about thinking merely at the level of 'how things went'; it is about looking for 'ways to make a difference', rendering explicit one's tacit knowledge and informal theories, and making the familiar strange. My own reflections toward deeper thinking centre on personal beliefs, persistence, the concept of care, conditions of 'turbulence' and asking questions.

Regarding personal beliefs, I was particularly affected by Dan Granger's advice to 'know what your centre is, and how to maintain that'. Staying grounded in a personal and articulated set of values in a world filled with competing agendas and waves of technological marketing can be difficult, especially when the time available to step back and reflect (in the Hillier sense) is fractured. One of the earlier generation of leaders in distance education, Kevin Smith from Australia, once reflected that his staff or students would never forgive him for 'insincerity, lack of consistency and lack of integrity'. The participants in this study knew what it means to be a principled professional. Reasoning one's way through highly conflictual situations, knowing in advance that some decisions will create difficulties or disadvantages for someone, is challenging, especially when working *de novo* – lacking knowledge of past experience. Learning that there is no room for self-serving or self-important behaviour in complex innovations or that some decisions have to be implemented with maximum courtesy helped the pioneers develop colleagueship. How far notions of respectful cooperation really operate in competitive academe will be something to watch.

Persistence – not giving in or giving up – and its associated qualities of determination and resilience – thread through many pioneer stories. A principle-driven professional sometimes has to respond to contextual conditions that create negative pressures or reveal oppositional values. Persistence to keep breaking new ground or constructing until a fine building emerges takes public courage and intrinsic motivation. Gisela Pravda's decades of a critical focus on equity in gender issues is one example. Other examples of principled persistence relate to the informed use of 'low' or non-disruptive, context-appropriate technologies, repeatedly telling the stories of learner success until university leaders and the national media finally listen, and insisting on rigorous academic standards. Hmmm: where in my own professional life is there evidence of persistence that shows courage, not stubbornness? When I hear yet another demonstration of technological 'bells and whistles', will I still ask the timeless questions about learning and teaching principles (or about 'old wine in new bottles'), knowing that such questions are not always welcome?

Roger Mills's concept of 'a culture of care' caught my ear, but not for its alliteration. That word 'care' is so multi-layered and loaded with expectations, not all of which may be congruent. More critical thinking is needed here: how does 'caring' resonate in today's market and commodity discourses? How far can I care without feeling disillusioned about some current attitudes of ultra-pragmatic, consumer-minded and time-challenged students, or those who expect high grades without much effort? Some days I cannot easily reconcile my response of caring with some expectations of students. Where, in a student's experience, might a teacher's caring and honesty appear conflictual? How many large postsecondary institutions today have the systemic flexibility to find whatever ad-hoc solutions are needed for diverse student needs?

David Murphy's reminders about the 'turbulence' that attends creativity helped me recall experiences that felt like whitewater rafting at the time. The intuitive and rapid design of audio-conferenced discussion tasks *in situ* – in the heat of my own thinking and my assessments of students' thinking – calls for reflection afterwards to answer the congruence questions that Barbara Spronk asks: 'What am I trying to do?' and 'What am I really doing?' Would differing answers necessarily indicate a lack of congruence between my 'talk' and my 'walk'? David Murphy's musings about the Open University (UK) being the possible 'fluctuation' that 'shattered the old ways and produced a new dissipative structure' for postsecondary education pushed me into some thoughts about possible long-term impacts of the latest information selection and aggregation technologies (via federated search engines and Really Simple Syndication – RSS – tools). And what kinds of creative turbulence do our learners and part-time tutors/teachers most need now? Are we willing to discuss the sources and outcomes of our own operational turbulence? Deliciously detailed stories of failure, retreat from an innovation or cancellation of projects usually do not create acceptably positive reports for administrators. But, as Patrick Guiton remarked, they may prompt constructive reflection inside one's professional self.

Framing questions to promote critical interrogation of a context, a principle, an experiential lesson or an intervention in learners' lives seems more important than ever, as Michael Collins argues. Focusing on the end users' conditions to guide decision-making about possible technology applications may seem obvious in the abstract but may be elusive in the everyday. As David Hawkridge might ask in a planning session: 'It's feasible, but is it desirable?' It is not usually easy or comfortable to ask critical questions that act as spades to dig into the 'ground' of hegemonic thinking. André Grace argues that 'critical adult education is preoccupied with how the field of study and practice might become more ethical, just, and inclusive [to] respond better to the needs and desires of adults who are mediating the demands of homeplace, learningplace, and workplace' (2006: 135). The 44 pioneers were thus preoccupied; but how far are today's discussions so oriented? Acknowledging some current trends toward privately-funded postsecondary flexible institutions will involve critical comparisons with the values and habits of traditional publicly-funded institutions. Asking how far the new information management technologies, especially in library services, may change students' perceptions of their own information literacies may reveal challenges to epistemological authority typically assumed by teachers and course designers.

The pioneers' lessons prompt me to rethink the 'laws of media'. Marshall and Eric McLuhan used a 'tetrad' of questions to help them interrogate any media innovation: 'What does it enhance or intensify?'; 'What does it render obsolete?'; 'What does it retrieve that was previously obsolesced?'; and 'What does it produce or become when pressed to an extreme?' (McLuhan and McLuhan 1988: 7). Email for almost every communication pushed aside handwritten, 'snail-mail' documents. Asynchronous online forms of learning pushed aside some time-bound classroom lectures and audioconferences.

Each innovation enhanced the reach, speed or frequency of contact, and significantly reduced the physical effort of being 'present' or needing to know the recipient's readiness. As email became ubiquitous, some of us reached back for the handwritten note to signify a really special communication. Taken to its extreme, what might a new mono-technology lead to? Perhaps the reverse of its original intentions? After this decade of asynchronous online activity, I now hear students asking for some changes: they want some asynchronous convenience but there is more: they also want synchronous discussions with 'real' colleagues. Are they reacting to some new tyrannies caused by a technology? Might some students prefer live discussions via reliable, high audio quality internet-based telephony, and others prefer face-to-face, time away from home/workplace sessions? Or mixes of the above? How far will my extensive lessons of audioconferencing in actual rooms transfer to electronic contexts, given that each technology's features produces its own mediation impacts? Might residential schools – this time in upscale facilities – become a helpful refuge from the everyday? Students want access to adequate information but they do not want to be swamped, so they look for intermediaries – electronic and human – to help them forage for and organize information. Does this looking create a new, subtle shift to increased roles for librarians, less dependency on predesigned course materials, and a reduction of the perceived added value of tutors?

Ultimately, and apart from reminders that I still need to articulate and 'walk my talk' about the principles in the first paragraph, are the findings of this study helpful to me? Absolutely. They help me integrate (Duffy and Orrill 2003) new understandings into a more explicit framework and re-challenge some current discourses. I hope the wisdom of the pioneers and the commentators is as useful to you.

References

Duffy, T.M. and Orrill, C. (2003) Constructivism, in A. Kovalchic and K. Dawson (eds) *Education and Technology: An Encyclopedia.* Santa Barbara, CA: ABC-CLIO.

Grace, A.P. (2006) Critical adult education: engaging the social in theory and practice, in T. Fenwick, T. Nesbit and B. Spencer (eds) *Contexts of Adult Education: Canadian Perspectives.* Toronto: Thompson Educational Publishing.

McLuhan, M. and McLuhan E. (1988) *Laws of Media: The New Science.* Toronto: The University of Toronto Press.

Part 5

Literature suggestions

Each interviewee could suggest one or two of their own publications (or of a colleague) of possible interest to readers and that are easy to locate and retrieve. Not all interviewees responded to the offer.

Bates, A.W. (1999) *Managing Technological Change: Strategies for College and University Leaders*. San Francisco, CA: Jossey-Bass.
Bates, A.W. (2005) *Technology, E-learning and Distance Education*, 3rd edn. London: Routledge.
Bernath, U. and Rubin, E. (eds) (2003) *Reflections on Teaching and Learning in an Online Master Program: A Case Study*. Oldenburg: BIS-Verlag.
Bernath,U. and Szücs, A. (eds) (2004) *Supporting the Learner in Distance Education and E-Learning*, Proceedings of the Third EDEN Research Workshop, Carl von Ossietzky University of Oldenburg, Germany, March 4–6, 2004. Oldenburg: BIS-Verlag, www.uni-oldenburg.de/zef/mde/series/.
Carr, R., Jegede, O., Wong T-M. and Yuen, K-S. (eds) (1999) *The Asian Distance Learner*. Hong Kong: Open University of Hong Kong Press.
Coats, M. (1994) *Women's Education*. Buckingham: The Society for Research into Higher Education and Open University Press.
Coats, M. and Stevenson, A. (2005) *Reflective Practice in Open and Distance Learning: How Do We Improve?* Paper presented at the 11th Cambridge International Conference on Open and Distance Learning, Cambridge, www.open.ac.uk/cobe/publications.htm, accessed 30 November 2006.
Cowan, J. (2004) Beyond reflection: where next for curricula which concentrate on abilities? in C. Baillie and I. Moore (eds) *Effective Learning and Teaching in Engineering*. London: Routledge/Falmer.
Cowan, J. (2006) *On Becoming an Innovative University Teacher*, 2nd edn. Maidenhead: Open University Press.
Faith, K. (ed.) ([1988] 2000) *Toward New Horizons for Women in Distance Education: International Perspectives*. London: Croom Helm. Reissued in 2000 by University of London (UK).
Farrell, G. (ed.) (2001) *The Changing Faces of Virtual Education*, www.col.org/colweb/site/pid/3335, accessed 1 December 2006.

Farrell, G.M. (ed.) (2004) *ICT and Literacy: Who Benefits? Experiences from Zambia and India,* www.col.org/colweb/site/pid/3104#, accessed 1 December 2006.

George, J., Cannell, C., Cowan, J. and Hewitt, L. (2004) Failure dances to the tune of insecurity: affective issues in the assessment and evaluation of access learning, *Journal of Access Policy and Practice,* 1: 119–33.

George, J.W. (2002) Action research: development for staff and students, *Journal of Distance Education,* 17(1): 47–62.

Gibson, C. (2003) Learners and learning: theoretical foundations, in M.G. Moore and W.G. Anderson (eds) *Handbook of Distance Education.* Mahwah, NJ: Lawrence Erlbaum Associates.

Gibson, C. (2007) From Chautauqua to correspondence to computers: non-formal education in transformation, in T. Evans, M. Haughey and D. Murphy (eds) *The World Handbook of Distance Education.* London: Elsevier.

Granger, D.W. (1993) Reflections on curriculum as process, in T. Evans and D. Nation (eds) *Reforming Open and Distance Education.* London: Kogan Page.

Granger, D. and Bowman, M. (2003) Constructing knowledge at a distance, in M.G. Moore, and W.G. Anderson (eds) *Handbook of Distance Education.* Mahwah, NJ: Lawrence Erlbaum Associates.

Guiton, P. (1992) Murdoch University: interlocking the learning modes, in I. Mugridge (ed.) *Distance Education in Single and Dual Mode Universities.* Vancouver: The Commonwealth of Learning.

Harry, K. (ed.) (1999) *Higher Education Through Open and Distance Learning* (Vol. 1 of *World Review of Distance Education and Open Learning*). London: Routledge.

Hawkridge, D. (2002) Distance learning and instructional design in international settings, in J. Dempsey and R. Reiser (eds) *Trends and Issues in Instructional Design and Technology.* Englewood Cliffs, NJ: Prentice-Hall.

Hawkridge, D. (2003) The human in the machine: reflections on mentoring at the British Open University, *Mentoring and Tutoring,* 11(1): 15–24.

Hope, A. and Guiton, P. (eds) (2005) *Strategies for Sustainable Open and Distance Learning* (Vol. 6 of *World Review of Distance Education and Open Learning*). London: Taylor & Francis/Commonwealth of Learning.

Jenkins, J. (1980) *Materials for Learning.* London: Routledge & Kegan Paul.

Kenworthy, B.R. (1996) Distance education in Mongolia's political and economic transition, in T. Evans and D. Nation (eds) *Opening Education: Policies, Practices and Technologies in an Era of Globalization.* London: Routledge.

Kenworthy, B.R. (2002) Supporting the student in new teaching and learning environments, in R. Mills and A. Tait (eds) *Rethinking Learner Support in Distance Education.* London: Routledge.

Lambert, M. (2005) DETC: Pioneering and leading the distance learning sector, *Career Education Review,* April.

Latchem, C. and Hanna, D. E. (2001) *Leadership for 21st Century Learning: Global Perspectives from Leading Innovators.* London: Kogan Page.

Latchem, C. and Lockwood, F. (eds) (1998) *Staff Development in Open and Flexible Learning.* London: Routledge.

Lockwood, F.G. (ed.) (1994) *Materials Production in Open and Distance Learning.* London: Paul Chapman Publishing.

Lockwood, F.G. (1998) *Design and Production of Self-Instructional Materials.* London: Kogan Page.

Matthewson, C. (1994) Whose development, whose needs? Distance education practice and politics in the South Pacific, *Journal of Distance Education,* 9(2): 35–47.

Matthewson, C. and Thaman, K.H. (1998) Designing the *Rebbelib*: staff development in a Pacific multi-cultural environment, in C. Latchem and F. Lockwood (eds) *Staff Development Issues in Open and Flexible Education*. London: Routledge.

McIntosh, N. (1974) The evaluation of multi-media systems – some problems, *British Journal of Educational Technology*, 5(3): 43–59.

McIntosh, N.E., with Calder, J.A. and Swift, B. (1976) *A Degree of Difference: A Study of the First Year's Intake of Students to the Open University of the United Kingdom*. Guildford: Society for Research into Higher Education at the University of Surrey.

Mills, R. (1999) Diversity, convergence and the evolution of student support in higher education in the UK, in A. Tait, and R. Mills (eds) *Patterns of Flexibility for the Individual Learner: The Convergence of Open and Distance Learning and Conventional Education*. London: Routledge.

Mills, R. (2004) Looking back, looking forward: what have we learned? in J.E. Brindley, C. Walti and O. Zawacki-Richter (eds) *Learner Support in Open, Distance and Online Learning Environments*. Oldenburg, Germany: Bibliotheks-undInformationssystem der Universität Oldenburg.

Moran, L. and Mugridge, I. (eds) (1993) *Collaboration in Distance Education: International Case Studies*. London: Routledge.

Moran, L. and Rumble, G. (eds) (2004) *Vocational Training through Distance Education: A Policy Perspective*. London: Routledge.

Mugridge, I. (1981) The establishment of a new distance learning institution: the Open Learning Institute of British Columbia, *Distance Education*, 2(1): 98–109.

Mugridge, I. (1986) The Open Learning Institute, in I. Mugridge and D. Kaufman (eds) *Distance Education in Canada*. London: Croom Helm.

Murphy, D., Carr, R., Taylor, J. and Wong, T-M (eds) (2004) *Distance Education and Technology: Issues and Practice*. Hong Kong: Open University of Hong Kong Press.

Nation, D. (2003) Globalization and the reinvention of distance education, in M.G. Moore and W.G. Anderson (eds) *The Handbook of Distance Education*. Mahwah, NJ: Lawrence Erlbaum Associates.

Perraton, H. (2000) *Open and Distance Learning in the Developing World*. London: Routledge.

Perraton, H. and Creed, C. (2001) *Applying New Technologies and Cost-effective Delivery Systems in Basic Education (Thematic Study for Education for All 2000 Assessment)*. Paris: UNESCO.

Perry, W. (1976) *Open University: A Personal Account*. Milton Keynes: Open University Press.

Poley, J. (2000) Leadership in the age of knowledge, in D.E. Hanna *et al.*, *Higher Education in an Era of Digital Competition: Choices and Challenges*. Madison, WI: Atwood.

Poley, J. (2001) The American Distance Education Consortium: from rural provision to virtual organization, in C. Latchem and D.E. Hanna (eds) *Leadership for 21st Century Learning: Global Perspectives from Educational Innovators*. London: Kogan Page.

Robinson, B. and Latchem, C. (eds) (2003) *Teacher Education Through Open and Distance Learning* (Vol. 3 of *World Review of Distance Education and Open Learning*). London: Routledge/Falmer.

Rumble, G. (1992) Explanation, theory and practice in distance education, in G.E. Ortner, K. Graff and H. Wilmersdoerfer (eds) *Distance Education as Two-way Communication: Essays in Honour of Börje Holmberg*. Frankfurt am Main: Verlag Peter Lang.

Rumble, R. (1997) *The Costs and Economics of Open and Distance Education.* London: Kogan Page.

Thomas, J. (1996) *Distance Education for Refugees: The Experience in Africa, 1980–1995.* Cambridge: International Extension College.

Thomas, J.H. (2001) *Audio for Distance Education and Open Learning: A Practical Guide for Planners and Producers.* Vancouver/Cambridge, UK: Commonwealth of Learning/International Extension College, www.col.org/colweb/site/pid/3152, accessed 4 December 2006.

Warr, D. (1992) *Distance Teaching in the Village: A Case Study of Basic Functional Education for Rural Development (Allama Iqbal Open University).* Cambridge: International Extension College.

Young, M., Perraton, H., Jenkins, J. and Dodds, T. (1980) *Distance Teaching for the Third World: The Lion and the Clockwork Mouse.* London: Routledge.

Index

The Society for Research into Higher Education

The Society for Research into Higher Education (SRHE), an international body, exists to stimulate and coordinate research into all aspects of higher education. It aims to improve the quality of higher education through the encouragement of debate and publication on issues of policy, on the organization and management of higher education institutions, and on the curriculum, teaching and learning methods.

The Society is entirely independent and receives no subsidies, although individual events often receive sponsorship from business or industry. The Society is financed through corporate and individual subscriptions and has members from many parts of the world. It is an NGO of UNESCO.

Under the imprint *SRHE & Open University Press*, the Society is a specialist publisher of research, having over 80 titles in print. In addition to *SRHE News*, the Society's newsletter, the Society publishes three journals: *Studies in Higher Education* (three issues a year), *Higher Education Quarterly* and *Research into Higher Education Abstracts* (three issues a year).

The Society runs frequent conferences, consultations, seminars and other events. The annual conference in December is organized at and with a higher education institution. There are a growing number of networks which focus on particular areas of interest, including:

Access	FE/HE
Assessment	Graduate Employment
Consultants	New Technology for Learning
Curriculum Development	Postgraduate Issues
Eastern European	Quantitative Studies
Educational Development Research	Student Development

Benefits to members

Individual

- The opportunity to participate in the Society's networks
- Reduced rates for the annual conferences
- Free copies of *Research into Higher Education Abstracts*
- Reduced rates for *Studies in Higher Education*

- Reduced rates for *Higher Education Quarterly*
- Free online access to *Register of Members' Research Interests* – includes valuable reference material on research being pursued by the Society's members
- Free copy of occasional in-house publications, e.g. *The Thirtieth Anniversary Seminars Presented by the Vice-Presidents*
- Free copies of *SRHE News* and *International News* which inform members of the Society's activities and provide a calendar of events, with additional material provided in regular mailings
- A 35 per cent discount on all SRHE/Open University Press books
- The opportunity for you to apply for the annual research grants
- Inclusion of your research in the *Register of Members' Research Interests*

Corporate

- Reduced rates for the annual conference
- The opportunity for members of the Institution to attend SRHE's network events at reduced rates
- Free copies of *Research into Higher Education Abstracts*
- Free copies of *Studies in Higher Education*
- Free online access to *Register of Members' Research Interests* – includes valuable reference material on research being pursued by the Society's members
- Free copy of occasional in-house publications
- Free copies of *SRHE News* and *International News*
- A 35 per cent discount on all SRHE/Open University Press books
- The opportunity for members of the Institution to submit applications for the Society's research grants
- The opportunity to work with the Society and co-host conferences
- The opportunity to include in the *Register of Members' Research Interests* your Institution's research into aspects of higher education

Membership details: SRHE, 76 Portland Place, London
W1B 1NT, UK Tel: 020 7637 2766. Fax: 020 7637 2781.
email: srheoffice@srhe.ac.uk
world wide web: http://www.srhe.ac.uk./srhe/
Catalogue: SRHE & Open University Press, McGraw-Hill
Education, McGraw-Hill House, Shoppenhangers Road,
Maidenhead, Berkshire SL6 2QL. Tel: 01628 502500.
Fax: 01628 770224. email: enquiries@openup.co.uk –
web: www.openup.co.uk